Barcode at the back

ADVANCED MEDIA PLANNING

ADVANCED MEDIA PLANNING

by

JOHN R. ROSSITER
Australian Graduate School of Management

and

PETER J. DANAHER
University of Auckland, New Zealand

KLUWER ACADEMIC PUBLISHERS
Boston/Dordrecht/London

Distributors for North, Central and South America:
Kluwer Academic Publishers
101 Philip Drive
Assinippi Park
Norwell, Massachusetts 02061 USA

Distributors for all other countries:
Kluwer Academic Publishers
Distribution Centre
Post Office Box 322
3300 AH Dordrecht, THE NETHERLANDS

Library of Congress Cataloging-in-Publication Data

A C.I.P. Catalogue record for this book is available from
the Library of Congress.

To my Mother, Olive, with love.
J.R.R.

To my wife, Felicity, and children,
James and Cecily.
P.J.D.

TABLE OF CONTENTS

PREFACE

This book is a "how to and why" presentation of advanced media planning. It is intended for marketing managers who are responsible for advertising and for professional media planners in advertising agencies and media-buying specialist companies. Approximately 90 percent of advertising dollars are spent in media and this is a good reason for marketing managers to acquire a sound understanding of media planning. Media planners, the professionals, should need no urging to increase their knowledge in today's complex media world. And although this book provides an advanced approach to media planning, the basics are covered as well, making the book suitable for trainees.

Much of the strategic thinking in this book comes from the first author's comprehensive advertising text (Rossiter and Percy 1997), which is a useful companion volume, and readers of that book will recognize some of the material. The opportunity to work with Peter Danaher, a specialist media modeler, provided the impetus for the present book. It extends the strategic ideas and offers far more detailed coverage of media plan implementation. Peter also contributed the media planning computer software, Media Mania, supplied with this book.

Media planning consists of (1) formulating a media strategy to deliver the creative so as to best meet the brand's advertising objectives, and then (2) implementing the strategy in an accurate and cost-effective manner. Why "advanced" media planning? Media planning is still too conventional (Priemer 1986, 1987, 1989, 1990) and advancement is needed (Rossiter and Percy 1987, 1997) along the following lines. (1) Media strategy, at a basic level, comprises the joint decisions of who or whom to reach (loosely called "reach") and how often to reach them in terms of number of exposures (loosely called "frequency"). While reach and frequency are not incorrect, they are certainly too simplistic for modern media planning. This book introduces the advanced concept of reach patterns in making the reach decision, and develops the advanced concept of effective frequency in making the frequency decision. Reach patterns are an entirely new concept. Effective frequency, while not new, needs proper definition and an operational formula for its calculation, both of which are provided here. Other new concepts are also introduced and shown to be necessary for choosing an appropriate media strategy. (2) Media plan implementation, the other half of media planning, has become somewhat of a mathematical science. Nevertheless, if managers have put thought and effort into developing the media strategy, then they should want to be sure that it is accurately implemented. This requires the marketing manager to gain a hands-on understanding of media selection and of how media implementation models work. Most media planners use proprietary computer programs for media plan implementation which are probably not as accurate as more recent models. This book addresses implementation firstly from a qualitative "strategic rules" perspective, showing broadly how to construct the plan to achieve the media strategy. Implementation of the media plan is then considered quantitatively, with the aid of new media models developed by the second author.

This book therefore aims to promote a better—indeed advanced—understanding of media strategy and implementation for marketing managers and media planners.

The book consists of seven chapters, a computer software disk for the media models, and a user-manual appendix. Effectively, the presentation is in two parts corresponding with the two overall stages of media planning: media strategy (Chapters 1 to 4) and media plan implementation (Chapters 5 to 7 and Appendix). In the first chapter, new strategic definitions are presented which can replace many traditional media concepts, and the fundamental trade-offs in media planning are reviewed. The second explains reach patterns. The third defines effective frequency and then provides a formula for the estimation of minimum effective frequency for particular advertising situations. The fourth looks at effective reach and carryover, as well as tactical changes in frequency requirements. The fifth covers media selection, which is the choice between media types, and also the use of more than one medium when multiple media are thought to be the most effective choice for a campaign. The sixth discusses media data for media vehicles, and specifies strategic rules for achieving the media strategy via vehicle selection. In the seventh chapter, computer-model implementation of the plan is explained. This chapter is followed by the user-manual appendix for the book's media planning computer disk.

Thanks are due to Julie Kaczynski, Kluwer's business acquisitions editor, Dordrecht, who was the authors' encouraging and patient advocate, to Jo Groom, Kirsty Davies, Rebecca Butcher, Mary O'Sullivan, and Jocelyn Sorensen for their superb work on the book's manuscript and production, and to Michael Tantrum for computer programming.

ACKNOWLEDGEMENTS

The authors and publisher wish to acknowledge the co-operation of McGraw-Hill publishers (The McGraw-Hill Companies, Inc.) in granting permission to draw material from the book by John R. Rossiter and Larry Percy, *Advertising Communications & Promotion Management*, 2nd edition, New York: McGraw-Hill, 1997.

The authors also wish to acknowledge the assistance of a research grant from the American Academy of Advertising to the first author in 1988-89 which enabled this work to begin. Here is the publication from it.

CHAPTER 1

MEDIA STRATEGY: AN INTRODUCTION

Media planning consists of media strategy and implementation of that strategy in the media plan. This chapter introduces media strategy. It starts with the basics and then develops the advanced approach from these.

The advanced tasks of media strategy are to decide on the reach pattern for the advertising (or promotion) campaign and to calculate the required effective frequency levels throughout the campaign. The advanced perspective requires new concepts to be defined to represent the advanced parameters in media planning, and clarified definitions of some current concepts. The nature of, and the need for, the new concepts will become apparent after reviewing the basic parameters of the media plan.

1.1. Basic Parameters of the Media Plan

A media plan has three basic parameters: reach, frequency, and the number of advertising cycles for the year. Parameters are quantities that can take on different numerical values depending on the particular situation or application. In a media plan, numerical values have to be decided for reach, frequency, and the number of advertising cycles.

These basic parameters are shown in Figure 1.1 as the "media balloon" (Rossiter and Percy 1987, 1997). The balloon is composed of three "ears." If the balloon is "tied off" (representing a fixed media budget), the manager cannot make one ear of the balloon larger without squeezing at least one of the other two ears. If the manager could "inflate" the balloon to any necessary size (representing an unlimited media budget) then all three ears would enlarge, making possible an ideal media plan. In most advertising situations, however, the reality is that the media balloon will have a fixed size, constrained by the media budget set for the campaign. The budget constraint necessitates trade-offs between the three ears of the balloon—that is, between reach and frequency, reach and the number of advertising cycles, and frequency within each advertising cycle.

These basic trade-offs are discussed next. The principle that governs these trade-offs actually depends on an advanced parameter, effective frequency, but it can be stated simply as follows. *It is better to sell some people completely than many people not at all.*

1.1.1. REACH VERSUS FREQUENCY

A media plan with a fixed budget can be strategically designed to reach a lot of people a few times, or a few people a lot of times. This is the trade-off between reach and frequency.

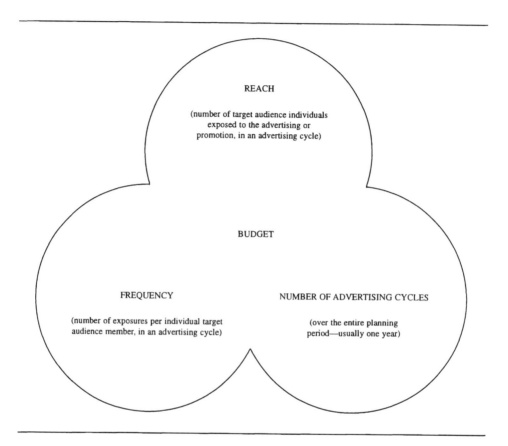

Figure 1.1. The "media balloon" showing the basic parameters of the media plan.

Suppose the media strategy calls for an emphasis on reach. By scattering the budget, and hence the advertising or promotion exposures, across a lot of different media types (such as TV, radio, newspapers, magazines, outdoor, a website, and promotion media) and across many different media vehicles (such as different TV programs, radio stations, and forms of promotions), a large number of different people will be exposed to the advertising but each person will not be exposed very often.

Alternatively, suppose the media strategy calls for an emphasis on frequency. By spending the same budget in only one media type, such as magazines, and in very few vehicles, such as *Fortune* and *Forbes* magazines, a much smaller number of people will be exposed to the advertising, but they will be exposed very frequently.

The reach and frequency trade-off applies similarly to media strategy for promotions. Take coupons as an example. The reach of a coupon plan could be emphasized by distributing them via a broad-audience medium such as newspapers and inserting the coupon once. The frequency of a coupon plan, a strategy that might be intended to reward loyal customers, could be emphasized by distributing the coupons regularly on or in the package, or, for a service, at the retail service outlet.

1.1.2. GEOGRAPHIC REACH VERSUS FREQUENCY

Reach is ultimately, of course, a geographic parameter. At one extreme, a campaign could attempt global reach, though not even satellite television or the Internet comes anywhere near achieving this yet. At the other, the campaign could be very local, as for a local retailer, or numerically sparse, as for a specialized small manufacturer.

The most common geographic reach and frequency trade-off is for the multi-regional marketer, who must often decide whether to apply a full media plan to just some of the regions or to reduce frequency in some regions so as to afford to reach all of them. For *new* products, this geographic trade-off is often applied in the strategy of a *national* or *multinational rollout* of the new product, with the frequency being adjusted as the manager observes what has happened in the initial market or markets. For *established* products, frequency may be deliberately set low in some regions (or demographic or psychographic markets) and high in others, depending on *competitive* strengths and weaknesses in those regions or markets. Schroer (1990) provides a sophisticated version of this strategy, based on varying the total advertising weight by region or market, but the actual variation is in frequency.

Reach versus frequency is the most typical trade-off in the media plan. As will be seen in the next several chapters, this trade-off is dictated by the media *strategy* that goes into the media plan.

1.1.3. REACH VERSUS NUMBER OF ADVERTISING CYCLES

The next most typical trade-off is between reach and the number of advertising cycles in the planning period (usually one year). As will become evident in the next chapter, this trade-off depends on the *reach pattern* selected for the media plan. Even if the media budget is very large, it is in most advertising situations unnecessary to reach everyone in the target audience continuously throughout the year. Rather, the year is judgmentally divided into a number of advertising *cycles* (ranging from as short as one hour for retail advertising up to three months in length or duration for manufacturers' advertising) in which advertising or promotions are to be placed. Of course, if the chosen cycles are close together, then this amounts to continuous advertising.

If the reach pattern indicates to advertise (or promote) in many short, closely-spaced cycles, as with a frequently-purchased product or service, then, for a fixed budget, reach will have to be reduced. For instance, a marketer employing a direct-response, databased program for low-cost products or services that are frequently bought would return to the same "proven prospects" relatively continuously rather than always trying to extend the reach to everybody on the list. Loyalty marketing programs to databased "club" members fit the extreme of this trade-off: low reach but many advertising cycles. In contrast, the marketer of an infrequently-purchased product or service would adopt a broad-reach media plan and advertise only occasionally, with just several advertising cycles a year, relying on the advertising's communication effects "carrying over" between cycles. This may be sufficient to keep long-term target audience individuals "interested" (brand aware and favorably disposed in terms of brand attitude) without having to reach them continuously. Indeed, continuous advertising might be overkill and a waste of the budget. Advertising for consumer durables, many industrial products, and also corporate image advertising and publicity would be likely examples of this high reach-but-few-advertising cycles option.

1.1.4. FREQUENCY VERSUS NUMBER OF ADVERTISING CYCLES

The third possible trade-off is between frequency *per* advertising cycle and the number of cycles in which to advertise (or promote). In the advanced media strategy approach, which is based on the reach pattern and a minimum level of frequency per advertising cycle, this is not always a possible trade-off. Because the media plan has to adhere to the reach pattern, and because the reach pattern has a fixed number of cycles each of which must deliver the appropriate minimum level of frequency to the individuals reached, it is the amount of reach that must be traded off instead. For instance, suppose it has been determined that the optimal media plan has to deliver a frequency of 2 exposures to each target audience individual every 4 weeks to prevent the typical individual from switching to another brand. If the media budget is limited, so that you can't reach everyone in the target audience at that frequency throughout the year, then you would have to settle for reaching as large a proportion of them as you can afford, to keep as many customers as possible. Consider what the assumptions imply. You would lose any individual who receives less than 2 exposures in a 4-week cycle, so reducing frequency per cycle is not an option, and you would lose all individuals who miss a cycle, so reducing the number of cycles is not an option. You have to reduce reach.

However, there is a trade-off to be made between frequency and number of advertising cycles when the media plan employs a *carryover* reach pattern. Because the frequency in each cycle, or more precisely the exposures in each cycle, is or are meant to last beyond the cycle, a difficult calculation has to be made regarding fewer advertising cycles, each one "loaded" with extra frequency so as to carry over longer, or more cycles containing less frequency but with shorter hiatuses between them. This calculation is discussed in Chapter 4.

Summary So Far
Reach, frequency, and number (length and spacing) of advertising cycles are the basic parameters whose numerical values must be decided in constructing the media plan. Ideally, the media budget should be established without a pre-set limit by using the *task method* (see Rossiter and Percy 1997). This method attempts to estimate the advertising expenditure that will be needed to achieve or guarantee the sales goal set for the brand for the year. If this budget amount were in fact made available, then no trade-offs or compromises would be necessitated in choosing the values of the parameters for the media plan: the manager or media planner would simply proceed to select the reach, frequency levels, and advertising cycles needed to get the task done. In the majority of advertising situations, however, this doesn't happen, either because upper management has placed a limit on the funds available for advertising, a limit which is rarely sufficient to achieve the task, or because managers put the task method estimation procedures into the "too-hard basket," a surprisingly common reaction but one that is becoming less

acceptable with the push toward advertising accountability. Whenever the budget is known to be limited, which is the usual case, then trade-offs have to be made.

The best trade-offs obviously depend on the media strategy for the target audience and the brand. But to decide on the best strategy, the manager or media planner has to understand several advanced parameters that can be employed within the media plan. These are explained next.

1.2. Advanced Media Plan Parameters

Definition of the parameters required for advanced media planning are provided in Table 1.1. This table lists definitions of all the relevant concepts for advanced media planning (to serve as a glossary). The *order* of the concepts in the table is meant to show how the advanced parameters develop from the basic parameters of reach and frequency, with reference to advertising cycles. The reach development and the frequency development are discussed in Sections 1.2.1 and 1.2.2 below, and are taken up in detail in the next three chapters.

1.2.1. REACH → INDIVIDUAL CONTINUITY → TIMING

Advanced media planning starts with the basic concept of reach and extends it in the form of individual continuity, which in turn can be extended to the precise timing of the ads or promotion offers delivered to the target audience. *Reach* refers to the number of target audience individuals exposed to the advertising or promotion, in an advertising cycle. Reach can be stated also as percentages of the target audience. However, it is preferable to keep the numerical reach firmly in mind because it is those numbers that have to be carried through (as in the task method) to calculate the media plan's effect on sales.

Individual continuity is the time-distribution of exposures, over successive advertising cycles in the planning period, for the typical target audience individual. It therefore represents frequency to the individual over the entire planning period but takes time *between* exposures into account. Individual continuity is the basis of the reach *patterns* introduced in the next chapter.

The concept of individual continuity, and its importance for media strategy, can be most easily seen by imagining yourself as a typical target audience prospect and answering a simple question: "How many times during the year would the advertiser have to reach me to interest me in trying this product, if I've not already tried it, and to keep me buying it?" The answer to this question may be "Once" if it is an infrequently-purchased product or service, such as insurance, or a fad product such as a new CD. More likely, though, the answer will be "At least several times," or possibly "Many times" for a product or service category that the individual purchases frequently and in which there are many brands on offer. From a media planning perspective, this is the notion of individual continuity.

Reach and individual continuity can be taken to an even more specific level with the media plan parameter of *timing*. The prospect's introspection would continue with a further question: "And when are the best times to reach me?" The answer would indicate opportunities to employ timing in the media plan.

TABLE 1.1. Media plan parameters and definitions

Parameter	Definition
Reach	The number of target audience individuals exposed to the advertising or promotion, in an advertising cycle. Reach, effective reach, and active effective reach (see definitions) can be expressed alternatively as percentages of the target audience, provided that the base number of target audience individuals is clearly specified.
Effective Reach	The number of target audience individuals reached at the effective frequency level in an advertising cycle.
Active Effective Reach	The number of target audience individuals who retain the effective frequency levels for a given duration after the previous advertising cycle. Active effective reach allows for *advertising carryover*.
Individual Continuity	The time-distribution of exposures, over successive advertising cycles in the planning period, for the *typical target audience individual*.
Reach Pattern	Distribution of individual continuity over target audience individuals so as to maximize effective reach and, if intended, active effective reach during the planning period.
Timing	Short-term individual continuity tactic whereby *media vehicles* are selected to deliver the advertising or promotion as close as possible to the occurrence of the target audience individual's category need or to the point of decision.
Frequency	The number of exposures per individual target audience member, in an advertising cycle.
Effective Frequency	The number of exposures, in an advertising cycle, believed or known to be able to maximize the target audience individual's disposition to purchase. Effective frequency is always expressed as a minimum effective frequency per cycle (MEF/c) and sometimes additionally with a maximum effective frequency beyond which additional exposures decrease disposition to purchase (MaxEF/c).
Advertising Carryover	The persistence of disposition to purchase caused by advertising exposures. Lack of persistence is advertising "decay." Mainly considered as persistence after an advertising cycle, within-cycle persistence is also relevant when exposures received are spaced in time. (Also see active effective reach.)
Dominance	Frequency tactic whereby the MEF/c is set higher than the frequency used by the largest competitor (called LC + 1 in the MEF/c formula) for one or more advertising cycles.

Advertising Cycle	A flight of advertising (or promotion) within the advertising period. The extremes are a continuous schedule in which there is one long advertising cycle equal to the entire period, though more typically the upper limit of cycle duration is three months; and a discontinuous schedule in which the advertising cycles may be as short as one day or even one hour.
Purchase Cycle	The average length of time, for the average target audience member, between purchases in the *category* (also known as the IPT or inter-purchase time, or IPI or inter-purchase interval).
Insertion	Placement of the ad or promotion offer in a media vehicle. The insertion represents an OTS (see definition) *only* to those people who are reached by the vehicle.
OTS	Opportunity(ies) to see (or hear or read) the ad or promotion offer. Used as a singular or plural term. Singular OTS is the same as an "exposure." Plural OTS is the same as frequency.
Exposure	Placement of the advertisement in a media vehicle that the target audience is *known or expected* to see, hear or read. Same as an OTS (see definition). Exposure is an *opportunity* for the target audience to pay attention to the ad but does not refer to actual attention.
Exposure Distribution	Frequency distribution of exposures in an advertising cycle, expressed as target audience percentages; thus the percentage exposed 0 times (that is, *not* reached), the percentage exposed exactly 1 time, the percentage exposed exactly 2 times, and so forth. Because the zero (unreached) cell is included, the percentage frequencies add to 100 percent of the target audience. Reach (see definition) is 100 minus the zero-cell percentage.
GRPs	Gross Rating Points, also referred to as "weight." The GRPs of a media schedule are the sum of the percentage reach of each advertising (or promotion) insertion in an advertising cycle. 1 GRP means that the insertion reaches 1 percent of the target audience; 10 GRPs means that the insertion reaches 10 percent; etc., with a maximum possible 100 GRPs for one insertion. The target audience on which the GRPs are based should be clearly specified. GRPs are usually calculated as the sum of the target audience ratings of every vehicle used in the advertising cycle, with multiple insertions in a vehicle receiving the vehicle's rating each time. Thus 3 insertions in a vehicle with a 10 rating is 30 GRPs, as is 3 insertions in three different vehicles each with a 10 rating. (Note that actual reach and frequency are lost in this gross sum. GRPs are an estimate of the total number of exposure opportunities, or OTS, per 100 target audience members, in an advertising cycle, without regard to whether the individuals receiving these OTS were the same people or different people.) GRPs apply to any and *all* advertising and promotional media and have the same definition universally.

| CPM | (Advertising) cost per thousand people reached. The M is from the Latin word *mille*, a thousand. If the people base is replaced by people representing just the target audience, then this becomes cost per thousand target individuals, or CPMT. |
| CPERP | (Advertising) cost per effective reach point. The cost per percentage (per 1 percent) of *effective* reach. Can be extended to include cost per active effective reach point during hiatus periods in carryover reach patterns. |

Timing is a short-term continuity tactic implemented by selecting *media vehicles* to deliver the advertising or promotion as close as possible to the occurrence of the target audience individual's category need or to his or her point of decision (Priemer 1986). In mass media, timing is very expensive to achieve. As will be reviewed in Chapter 5 in conjunction with media plan implementation, there is a whole class of point-of-decision (POD) media specialized for the purpose of timing. These are very important for *promotions*, which are usually most effective when delivered at the point of decision.

1.2.2. FREQUENCY → EFFECTIVE FREQUENCY → DOMINANCE

Frequency, at the individual level, should be "effective frequency." *Effective frequency* is the number of exposures, in an advertising cycle, believed or known to be able to maximize the target audience individual's *disposition to purchase* (Rossiter and Percy 1997, chapter 16). Those readers familiar with quantitative brand choice models may see that "disposition to purchase" is equivalent to the individual's *purchase probability* for the brand.

The most important number—actually a *series* of numbers, depending on the reach pattern—is the *minimum effective frequency* (MEF) at which the advertising or promotion offer will "start working" and below which it won't work at all. Exposures beyond the MEF level are still effective but they are unnecessary unless carryover beyond the intermediate cycle is intended (see Chapter 4). Individual ads *may*, with continued exposures, suffer loss of attention (especially in print media) or begin to incur the target audience's dislike (especially in broadcast media), either of which can cause disposition to decrease. If so, the number of exposures just before disposition starts to decrease is known as *maximum* effective frequency (MaxEF).

Effective frequency can be extended into another advanced parameter of the media plan called *dominance* (Broadbent 1979). Dominance is a frequency tactic whereby the MEF per advertising cycle (MEF/c) is set higher than the frequency used by the *leading competitor*. This dominance is then sustained for each advertising cycle, which may require cutting back on reach if the budget is fixed. In the MEF/c formula described in Chapter 3, dominance enters in the "LC + 1" component.

1.2.3. EFFECTIVE REACH

The parameters of reach and effective frequency, in an advertising cycle, are *combined* in the parameter of effective reach. *Effective reach* is the number of target audience individuals reached at the effective frequency level (MEF or higher) in an advertising cycle. An upper limit to effective frequency (MaxEF) may also be specified and, if so, effective reach is defined within the MEF to MaxEF range. Effective reach, in some plans together with active effective reach, explained below, is the most important parameter for evaluating a media plan as it evolves cycle by cycle.

1.2.4. ACTIVE EFFECTIVE REACH

For some campaigns, the advertising is expected to work within a short time after exposure, mainly within the advertising cycle in which it appears. Retail advertising is a good example of expected short-term effectiveness, and most direct-response advertising has immediate effects or none at all. For other campaigns, however, the advertising is expected to work both during the advertising cycle and for some length of time *afterwards*. The aftereffect is known as *advertising carryover*. For instance, a "burst" or flight of ads might run for a month: some people will buy the brand during that month and others will still remember the advertising (more precisely, they will retain its brand-related communication effects) up to some weeks afterwards and then buy the brand. To incorporate the carryover phenomenon, another new parameter is required, called active effective reach.

Active *effective reach* is the number of target audience individuals who *retain* the MEF level *beyond* the advertising cycle. Active effective reach is the means by which a media plan can produce advertising carryover. This in turn depends on the rate at which the communication effects of the ads in the cycle fade or "decay" (not the most pleasant word but one that is commonly used by media theorists, who in turn borrowed it from psychologists' research on learning and memory). For instance, if the MEF/c is determined to be 4 exposures in a 3-week cycle, individuals who received, say, 6 exposures may "lose a couple" of exposures (strictly speaking, lose a proportion of the effects of these exposures) in the ensuing week or two but still be at MEF two weeks later. The number or percentage of target audience individuals who are "still at MEF" at some designated interval after the advertising cycle has ended constitutes the "active" effective reach at that time. The active effective reach may be zero in the case of fast-fading ads, or it may remain close to the effective reach attained during the cycle in the case of a very persistent or "memorable" ad or series of ads, but not for an unlimited time, of course.

The so-called *flighting* types of reach patterns (see Chapter 2) depend on the assumption of strong carryover, that is, on achieving a high level of active effective reach. The actual, as contrasted with the assumed, carryover is quite difficult to measure. This will be covered theoretically in Chapter 4 and examined as an implementation issue in Chapter 7.

1.2.5. ADVERTISING CYCLE

An *advertising cycle* refers to a flight of advertising (or promotion) within the advertising period. The entire period (usually one year) is judgmentally divided into a number of discrete periods in which advertising or promotion insertions are made in the media plan. These insertion periods are often referred to as "flights" of advertising or promotion. The intervals *between* flights or advertising cycles are often known as *hiatus* periods.

The definition refers to a flight rather than to a particular duration because, in the case of some media such as magazines and direct mail, the time of the advertising insertion and the time when it is actually seen or read by the consumer may represent a long delay (Pincott 1990). From the media planner's perspective, the notion of a *flight of insertions* is equivalent to an advertising cycle.

There is no fixed time for an advertising cycle: it could, theoretically, be as long as one year in the case of a continuous advertising schedule (although three months is a more typical upper limit) or it may be as short as a day or even one hour in the case of, for example, a retail sales promotion. The duration of an advertising cycle—in practice —is determined by the time needed to get enough insertions into the media vehicles selected so as to attain the desired effective reach. This in turn depends on the reach pattern and whether it has a reach emphasis or a frequency emphasis. (Chapter 7 provides some illustrations.) Most commonly for fast-moving consumer goods (fmcg), the advertising cycles are 1 week to 4 weeks in duration.

A *purchase cycle*, a concept relevant in media planning for regularly-purchased products or services, refers to the average length of time, for the average target audience member, between purchases in the product or service *category*. The purchase cycle is also known as the IPT, inter-purchase time, or IPI, inter-purchase interval. Advertising cycles in media plans should be geared to purchase cycles if the product or service is one that is purchased frequently and at reasonably regular intervals.

Looking Ahead
These concepts and parameter definitions will come into play many times throughout the book, and the reader will find it helpful to use the glossary in Table 1.1 earlier. The rest of the first part of the book is devoted to the two major aspects of media strategy: the reach pattern (Chapter 2) and effective frequency (Chapters 3 and 4). The second part of the book deals with media plan implementation.

REACH PATTERNS

Deciding on an appropriate *reach pattern* for the media plan is the first of the two major decisions in media strategy. The reach pattern is defined (Chapter 1, Table 1.1) as the distribution of individual continuity over target audience individuals so as to maximize effective reach and, if intended, active effective reach during the planning period.

To decide the appropriate reach pattern, the manager or media planner has to look at the entire advertising and promotion schedule from the *individual* target prospect's viewpoint. In their 1987 book, Rossiter and Percy broke with tradition by defining key media terms such as "frequency" and "continuity" from the individual perspective. Priemer's (1986, p. 28) quotation encapsulates exactly the reason for the individual perspective: "Once we can visualize how to 'sell' one consumer, we are ready to reach out *effectively* for millions (but not before then)." The individual prospect with whom we are concerned is the *typical member of the target audience*.

Rossiter and Percy's second edition of their book (1997), following the pioneering work by Longman (1971), offered for the first time a classification of eight reach patterns from which the manager can choose. These consist of four reach patterns for new product media plans and four reach patterns for established product media plans. The manager or media planner should be able to find a reasonably good fit of *one* of these reach patterns, or in some cases a *sequence* of two reach patterns, to the present advertising or promotion situation and can then apply minor adaptations as necessary (see Chapter 4 in this book, which discusses short-term scheduling and timing). The reach patterns are presented and discussed next.

2.1. Reach Patterns for New Products

Reach patterns for *new products* are shown in Figures 2.1 through 2.4: the blitz pattern, the wedge pattern, the reverse-wedge/PI pattern, and the short fad pattern. In the diagrams, reach (of the target audience) is depicted by the vertical height of the blocks in the bar charts. The frequency, per flight, is depicted, on a relative basis, by the *width* or thickness of the bars. The horizontal axis is time over the advertising planning period, which marks advertising cycles.

2.1.1. BLITZ PATTERN

The ideal pattern for a new product or service, if you can afford it, consists of a "blitz" of continuous advertising for the first year (Figure 2.1). It is virtually impossible to over-advertise a new product or service during its introduction (Aaker and Carman

1982). The blitz pattern will maximize the first-mover advantage if your brand is the first in the category (Carpenter and Nakamoto 1989). However, it appears that blitz-level spending is also necessary if a later-entering brand hopes to overtake the market leader (Urban, Carter, Gaskin and Mucha 1986).

The blitz pattern aims for 100 percent reach of the target audience—regarding the advertising cycle as the full year—and packs in frequency, to every individual, at the rate of at least 1 exposure weekly, which would be 50 or more exposures for the year. One-plus exposure per week may not seem like much, but with 100 percent reach of the target audience, this is a lot of advertising. The blitz pattern will maximize the rate of trial (Lodish and Lubetkin 1992) and it should be kept in mind that new product trial can take up to two years before maximum penetration is attained (Artz 1991). The blitz pattern will also tend to suppress the effects of any competitors' advertising by use of sustained dominance.

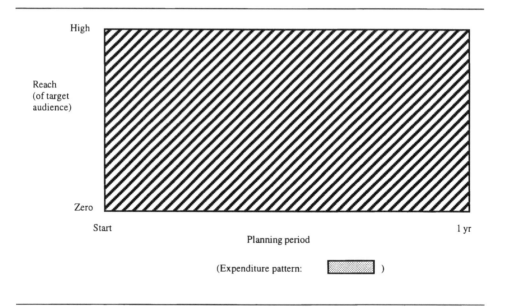

Figure 2.1. "Blitz" reach pattern (new products).

With the blitz pattern, the advertiser will need a fairly large "pool" of advertising executions, built around the same positioning strategy, to prevent advertising wearout, which is likely to be rapid with such a heavy schedule aimed at the same people. For informational products (see Chapters 3 and 5), a reasonably safe estimate is 2 to 4 executions. For transformational products, where ad likability is relevant, 4 to 6 executions may be needed to sustain a blitz.

It should be noted that the blitz pattern for *introductory promotions*, to gain trial, would usually occur only for the first six months because that is the length of time for which a product or service can legally use the description "new."

2.1.2. WEDGE PATTERN

The wedge pattern is probably the *most common* pattern for new product launches (despite the advantages of blitzing, as argued above). The "wedge" refers to the pattern of *expenditure*. The expenditure—translatable into GRPs in a given medium—begins like a blitz and then tapers off. For instance, for a new product launch, 400 GRPs a week may be bought for the first advertising cycle, tapering to 100 GRPs a week in the last cycle for the year. Note carefully, however, the inadequacy of GRPs as a media planning concept. The strategy in the wedge pattern (Figure 2.2) is not simply to taper the GRPs, but to keep the reach constant and taper the *frequency*. The typical target audience *individual* receives a succession of advertising flights—each with the same reach but successively declining frequency.

The wedge pattern can be considered as an alternative to a blitz when launching a *regularly-purchased* product or service. Not only high reach but heavy frequency is needed initially to create brand awareness for the new product and to enable prospective triers to learn the new product's benefits (informational advertising) or acquire its intended image (transformational advertising). Many of those who try the brand, if all goes well, will become favorable brand switchers or brand loyals who will require less frequency in later cycles to maintain their communication effects' status.

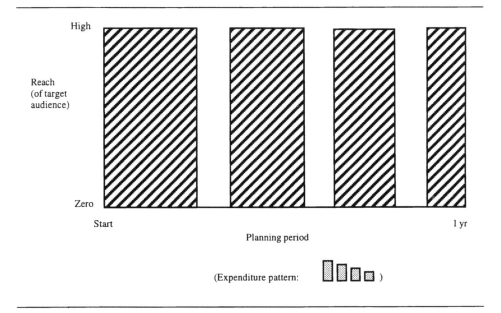

Figure 2.2. "Wedge" reach pattern (new products).
Width of bars indicates frequency.

With precise media placement—possible with media data that enables direct matching, as described in Chapter 6—the best reach pattern for a new brand in a regularly-purchased category would be to combine a blitz with a wedge, such that a blitz is continued against those who have not yet tried the brand, with trier-rejectors avoided, while a wedge is used for those who have tried it and have responded favorably. Direct matching in media vehicle selection (Garfinkle 1963; Winter 1980; Eskin 1985; Rossiter and Percy 1987, 1997; now more usually called "single-source" data and described in Chapter 6, Section 6.1.4) can enable this composite reach pattern to be attempted in many cases.

2.1.3. REVERSE-WEDGE/PI PATTERN

The "reverse-wedge" refers to media *expenditures* or GRPs over the planning period rather than to exposures as received by the typical target audience individual (Figure 2.3). The target audience individual receives *increasing* frequency with each flight, and reach is held constant at 100 percent of the target audience. In the most effective application of this pattern, the target audience consists of innovators or lead users initially, and then is broadened to the mass market. For definition and identification of consumer innovators, see Midgley and Dowling (1978) and Robertson (1971). For industrial lead users, see von Hippel (1986) and Urban and von Hippel (1988). The PI (personal influence) part is explained below.

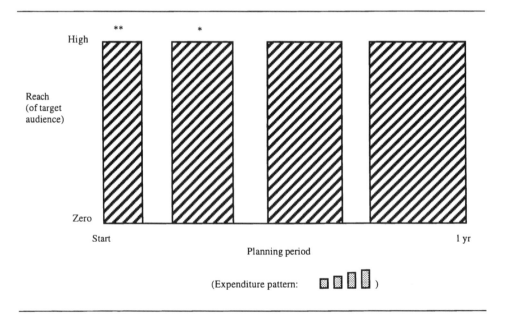

Figure 2.3. "Reverse-wedge/PI" reach pattern (new products). Width of bars indicates frequency. Asterisks denote innovator or lead user emphasis in target audience.

The reverse-wedge/PI pattern is most appropriate for the introduction of a new product or service in a category where *personal influence* (word of mouth, or visual influence in the event of products or services that are conspicuously consumed) is known to play an important role in brand adoption. The *low* initial advertising frequency will make the product or service appear to be somewhat "exclusive" (this works better still if the low frequency is accompanied by reach targeted only to *innovators* or *lead users*, many of whom will act as opinion leaders). As the hoped-for personal influence begins to spread, the advertising *frequency* is stepped up to help persuade the growing number of prospective adopters (in the innovator or lead user version of this pattern, the *reach* is also stepped up to now reach the mass market).

Personal influence is most likely for socially visible consumer products (see, for instance, Midgley and Dowling 1993). Apparently, the reverse-wedge/PI pattern was first used by Toohey's Brewery (now Lion Nathan) in Australia for the introduction of its Toohey's Red and, later, Toohey's Blue bitter beers. The reverse-wedge/PI strategy was very successful and has since been imitated, certainly in Australia, by almost all other new beer launches.

However, personal influence is also prevalent for industrial innovations, where there is definite pressure felt by firms to adopt the newest technology (see, for instance, Midgley, Morrison and Roberts 1992). The reverse-wedge/PI reach pattern is well worth investigating for the advertising of new industrial products.

2.1.4. SHORT FAD PATTERN

Some products are strictly "fad" products with a short product life cycle (Robertson 1971). Most are 1-time purchases, but others, such as inexpensive fashionwear or new toys, may be purchased more than once while the fad lasts.

The short fad reach pattern (Figure 2.4) is like a short blitz pattern. You have to get in early, during the *introduction* stage of the fad life cycle, and this calls for broad reach and high frequency; then the broad reach and high frequency need to be sustained (though this isn't for long with most fads) during the *growth stage* of the product life cycle in order to catch the large "middle majority" as they become ready to adopt the fad.

With a fad, the product category life cycle is so short that you have to blitz. The reverse-wedge/PI pattern is not an option even if there is personal influence stimulating the fad, as there often is, because this pattern's beginning is too narrow and too slow.

Examples of products that follow the short fad pattern include new movies (Weinberg 1994), "new" get-fit or weight-loss programs, and children's toys and games. The pattern is much less prevalent in industrial marketing.

2.2. Reach Patterns for Established Products

New products and services are exciting and important. If they survive, they become *established* products and services. Many of these rely on advertising and promotions to retain customers. (It should be noted that "relaunching" or "re-staging" an established product or service would count as a new product situation from a media strategy perspective and one of the above reach patterns should be used.)

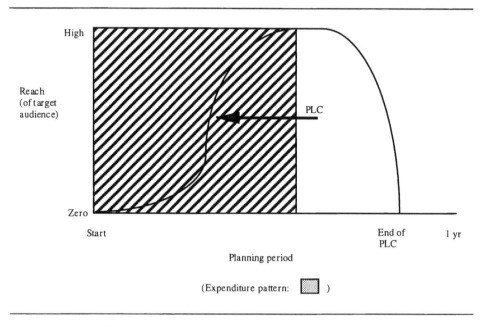

Figure 2.4. "Short-fad" reach pattern (fad products).

The alternative reach patterns for established products (and services) are shown in Figures 2.5 through 2.8 and are: the regular purchase cycle pattern, the awareness pattern, the shifting reach pattern, and the seasonal priming pattern.

2.2.1. REGULAR PURCHASE CYCLE PATTERN

Many products and services are purchased on a regular and relatively short purchase cycle, meaning that individuals are "in the market" at predictable intervals during the year. Most fast-moving consumer goods (fmcg) sold through supermarkets, drugstores and convenience outlets have a regular purchase cycle, as do many services such as drycleaning and health clubs. For instance, for fmcg products, U.S. data from Nielsen show that the average household purchases margarine every 19 days, toilet tissue every 20 days, tuna fish every 31 days, peanut butter every 48 days, and ketchup every 50 days (Helsen and Schmittlein 1992). Of course, these are averages and more precise surveys may show that particular demographic subgroups within the target audience follow shorter or longer purchase cycles for a particular product category, with singles living alone and large families buying in bulk probably being the two extremes.

The manager or media planner can take advantage of this regularity by designing the *advertising* cycle to coincide with the *purchase* cycle. Thus, instead of using some *standard period* for media planning (which traditionally is 4 weeks), it makes much better sense to gear the advertising to the purchase cycle because this is the true interval that the advertising (or promotion) has available to induce the consumer to switch brands. Of course, not every individual consumer starts at the same time and finishes at the same time even if his or her purchase cycle is exactly equal in duration to other consumers' purchase cycles. However, setting *frequency* on the basis of the *average* purchase cycle will tend to produce the right *rate* of advertising frequency for everyone.

In the diagram for the regular purchase cycle pattern (Figure 2.5), a purchase cycle of about 45 days is shown. Advertising has been placed in every second purchase cycle. Thus each of the four advertising cycles of 45 days is followed by a 45-day hiatus period. The rationale for this is explained at length, next.

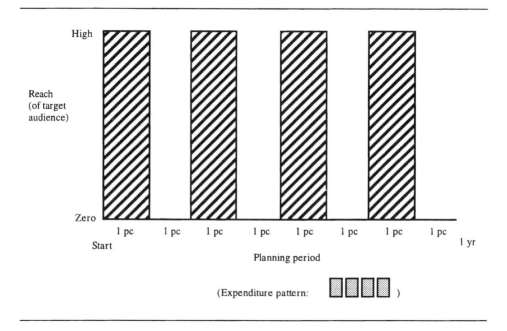

Figure 2.5. "Regular purchase cycle" reach pattern (established products with short, regular, purchase cycle). Width of bars indicates frequency *and* equals one purchase cycle.

The ideal reach pattern, with an unlimited budget, would be the blitz pattern (with varied execution of the ads). This would reach *every* target audience individual in *every* purchase cycle successively (that is, continuously throughout the year). On every purchase cycle, the buyer of a frequently-purchased product or service essentially *becomes a new prospect again* and is functionally a new individual to be reached even though he or she may have been reached before. Thus, the potential reach is 100 percent of prospects on *each* purchase cycle. Consider the 19-day purchase cycle for margarine, mentioned above. This means that there would be 19 purchase cycles of 19 days' duration (365 / 19 = 19, approximately) and that the yearly reach would potentially be 1900 percent! Fortunately, many prospects should become favorable brand switchers or loyal buyers—so they would require only minimal frequency in each purchase cycle. Nevertheless, few advertisers can afford to advertise continuously to all prospects.

The regular purchase cycle reach pattern is therefore shown as a *flighting* pattern. A flighting pattern within the regular purchase cycle reach pattern is actually more effective than continuous advertising (Lodish and Lubetkin 1992). The advantage of flighting is due to the well-documented phenomenon known as "hysteresis" (Little 1979) whereby a particular ad has its greatest purchase effect immediately, which then begins to fade even though the ad is continued (Eskin and Baron 1977; Haley 1978). The strategy is to stop an ad while it is still working but before fading occurs, and then run it again one or two purchase cycles later so it appears "new." In this manner, a continuous level of sales can be maintained even though the advertising is not continuous (also see Mahajan and Muller 1986; Mesak 1992).

In the off or "hiatus" purchase cycles, the brand's sales rate will still be maintained *to the extent that* there is advertising carryover (see Chapter 4), aided by purchase reinforcement among those who recently purchased the brand (Givon and Horsky 1990).

It is important to realize that the brand's retail promotions, too, form a media pattern in the same sense as the advertising pattern designed by the manufacturer for the brand. Retailers rarely promote a particular brand continuously, so they *de facto* achieve a flighted reach pattern for promotions for the brand such that its promotions usually occur several purchase cycles apart. Trade promotions can be used by the manufacturer to try to "regularize" this pattern.

2.2.2. AWARENESS PATTERN

The awareness reach pattern (Figure 2.6) applies to consumer and industrial products and services that have a *long purchase cycle* and a *long decision time*. Consumer examples would be long-haul holiday travel, new cars, and other luxury items. Industrial examples would include major equipment upgrades for businesses, tractors for farmers, and management consultancy services. These products or services are infrequently purchased—perhaps only once or only every several years—and are typically "pondered" for a long interval before the purchase decision is made. Always, nearly everyone in the target audience is "interested" or "semi-interested" in buying but, at any one time, only a few of these people actually decide to buy.

This reach pattern is called the "awareness" pattern (Longman 1971) because the strategy is to keep all prospects "aware" of the brand throughout the year, even though the time of purchase is unpredictable for any particular individual prospect. "Aware" is a loosely employed term in advertising; in fact, it means that the prospect has to have brand awareness *and* a favorable brand attitude (Rossiter and Percy 1987, 1997). Awareness is, essentially, disposition to purchase the brand, awaiting the prospect exceeding the threshold disposition to purchase in the *category*.

The awareness reach pattern aims for very high reach, to virtually all prospects, but relatively *low* frequency per advertising cycle, with the advertising cycles occurring at quite widely-spread intervals. Each of the advertising cycles has to contain an MEF level of insertions sufficient to sustain high *carryover* of the "awareness" (again, actually of brand awareness and brand attitude). The MEF/c formula is given in Chapter 3 but this reach pattern will require the *carryover* adjustment given in Chapter 4. This adjustment provides higher MEF per cycle so that the awareness (the brand disposition) will carry over between cycles. "Awareness" can be highly sensitive to competitive advertising, that is, to the advertised brand's "share of voice." This is indicated if the LC + 1 factor enters the MEF/c estimation (see Chapter 3). If so, "continuous tracking" survey research (Sutherland 1993) will be needed to properly implement this particular reach pattern—in terms of frequency, precisely, rather than reach which always aims to be as high as the budget permits.

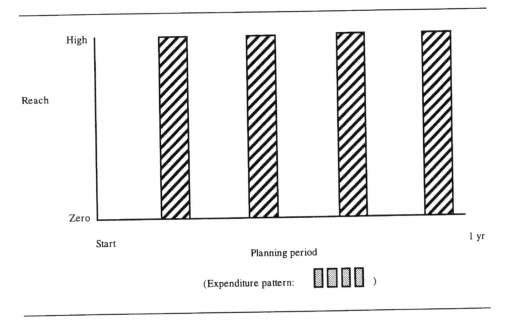

Figure 2.6. "Awareness" reach pattern (established products with long purchase cycle, long decision time). Width of bars indicates frequency.

A further refinement in implementing the awareness reach pattern for long purchase cycle long-decision products or services is to combine mass media advertising with direct-response ads (Woodside 1994). This can be accomplished with "double duty" direct-response ads, which serve a general communication effect or "image" advertising purpose as well as a direct-response purpose. An example is the cable TV commercials run in the U.S.A. by the Australian Tourist Commission, which always include an 800-number and website "super" on the screen at the end of the commercial which people can contact to obtain further information; after an inquiry is received, the ATC's U.S. office then mails to inquirers an Aussie travel booklet.

The awareness reach pattern can be used with double-duty ads for industrial products and services as well. These ads include a toll-free direct-response number, a reply coupon, or online reply and ordering details. Their dual purposes are to keep prospects aware and capture direct responses.

2.2.3. SHIFTING REACH PATTERN

The shifting reach pattern is appropriate for products and services with a long purchase
cycle and a *short* decision time.   Although the product or service may have a long
purchase cycle, the *decision* to buy is made very rapidly. On the one hand, the advertiser
would like the ads to be "out there" whenever a prospect's category need occurs and he
or she is thrust into the market; but, on the other hand, the advertiser cannot afford to be
out there all the time for everybody. Moreover, once an individual has bought, that
individual will be out of the market (a non-prospect) for a long time afterward. This
suggests shifting the reach.
       Examples of products and services that fit this pattern are home appliance
replacements, domestic carpet-cleaning, and office redecorating—activities that
consumers or businesses tend to put off until pushed into action by an emergency need
or until they are presented with a persuasive, problem-solving ad that is relevant to the
latent need. Whereas a Yellow Pages, other directory, or even a website ad might be
thought to be sufficient, aggressive companies in these categories will try to soak up
available demand with proactive media advertising.
       Direct-response (DR) advertising, especially 1-step DR ads that aim to make an
immediate sale, is also characterized as long purchase cycle, fast decision, in most
situations. The shifting reach pattern is ideal for DR ads.
       The shifting reach pattern is a rather unconventional one that regularly moves its focus
(Figure 2.7). The media plan successively scans 100 percent of prospects, but it does so
by moving from one group to another, seeking to persuade those within each group who
are in the market at that time. For instance, Figure 2.7 shows eight cycles, each of which
has a reach of about 12 percent, cumulating to about 100 percent before starting over.
       It is worth considering why the shifting reach pattern is preferable in the long
purchase cycle, short decision situation. The blitz pattern would be theoretically correct
in this situation but hardly affordable year in and year out over the long purchase cycle
of durables. The long purchase cycle, *long*-decision reach pattern, the awareness
pattern, is inappropriate because, firstly, it's not a long decision and, secondly, you want
to sell, not just make people aware, so heavy frequency (or equivalently, long or large
ads—see Chapter 3, Section 3.2.2 on ad unit adjustments to MEF/c) is required. The
shifting reach pattern is the appropriate compromise.
       In the shifting reach pattern, the main parameter value to decide is how short the
advertising cycles should be. Remember, each cycle has to be "filled with MEF" for that
group of the target audience that is reached in that cycle. It is tempting to "spread" the
length of the cycle so as to reach a large group of the target audience in each cycle,
whereas in fact the opposite is a better policy: short cycles with faster total audience
turnover. This is because product and service categories for which the shifting reach
pattern is advised tend to have very short decision times (direct responses) so that the
MEF spread over too long a cycle will be ineffective. Faster turnover of (smaller
portions of) the total audience also has the secondary benefit of forming a sort of
awareness reach pattern in that each audience-portion's hiatus will not be as long; this
is, however, a secondary consideration because those who buy will be "out of the
market" thereafter for a long time.

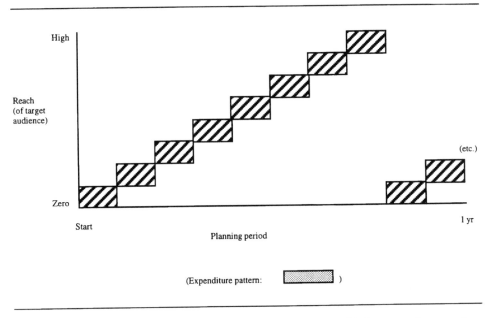

Figure 2.7. "Shifting" reach pattern (established products with long purchase cycle, *short* decision time). Width of bars indicates frequency.

Although reach pattern implementation is left till Chapter 6, the reader may be intrigued as to how the shifting reach is accomplished. It is implemented by concentrating the advertising in a small set of media vehicles for one advertising cycle, then changing to another *non-overlapping* small set of vehicles for the next advertising cycle, and so forth. For instance, advertising in the first cycle might be concentrated in early morning TV programs, then on lunchtime serials in the second cycle, early evening in the third, continuing through prime time and then late night programs in the final cycle. The audience overlap between these different time slots—even in a relatively "mass" medium like network television—is very small, so a shifting reach of new prospects will be achieved with each advertising cycle.

Larger advertisers may use different media types in each cycle to further shift the reach.

The shifting reach pattern also has advantages for the manufacturer and the retailer by *evening out* sales over the year.

2.2.4. SEASONAL PRIMING PATTERN

The seasonal priming reach pattern is appropriate for products and services whose sales are characterized by one, and sometimes two or three, large seasonal peaks (Figure 2.8). Low purchase-risk products are often distinctly seasonal, such as sunscreen products, hay fever remedies, and barbecue condiments. High purchase-risk seasonal purchases would include snowboarding or ski equipment, home swimming pools, and tax consultancy

services. Some products have more than one seasonal peak in the year, such as sunglasses
for the snow season and the summer, and of course traditional holiday greeting cards.

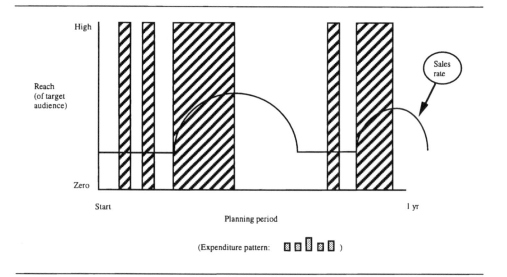

Figure 2.8. "Seasonal priming" reach pattern (established products with one or
several seasonal sales peaks—two shown here for illustration). Width of bars
indicates frequency. The thinner bars represent pre-seasonal primes.

It is obvious that a seasonal brand's advertising should reach people near (just prior
to or early into) the seasonal peak, because it will reach people when their category need
is strong and thus when they are ready to learn or be reminded about brand differences.
However, most other competitors will have adopted the same media strategy, so there
will be a lot of competitive advertising around the peak. The seasonal *priming* reach
pattern puts in a couple of flights of high reach but low frequency advertising a month
or two *before* the seasonal peak develops (Strong 1977).

Pre-seasonal advertising will "prime" seasonal advertising, moving consumers toward
the effective frequency level that will be needed for the brand *during* the peak. This early
priming, of course, reaches people in a low state of category need, so it won't sell the
product. What it will do is create brand awareness without competitive interference. The
primes may also begin to teach consumers the brand's message, although it is expected
that they will not show full interest until the seasonal advertising starts.

2.3. Combining Reach Patterns

One reach pattern may be sequentially "segued" into a second reach pattern within the
media-plan period. For instance, for a new fmcg brand, a blitz pattern may be used for
the first three months, to be followed by a regular purchase cycle pattern thereafter. Or
a reverse-wedge/PI pattern may be followed by an awareness reach pattern.

For established brands, the main variation is likely to be a seasonal or other promotional "push" overlay on either the regular purchase cycle, the awareness, or the shifting reach pattern. These pushes would be a reach and frequency increase, a frequency increase, and a reach increase, respectively, which are logical if you think about them. The reach and frequency increase would extend the regular purchase cycle reach pattern to less loyal prospects. The frequency increase in the awareness reach pattern, rather than just maintaining awareness, would accelerate disposition for a while. The reach increase in the shifting reach pattern would reach more prospects on that shift.

The eight reach patterns are fundamental template patterns that can be modified by thoughtful pre-planning of the media plan.

2.4. Summary Perspective

Think firstly about what you are trying to do with advertising and promotions at the *individual* level (imagine *yourself* in the role of the typical prospective customer). This individual prospect perspective is essential for identifying an appropriate reach pattern for the media plan. Think secondly that there are a lot of individual prospects to be reached (besides yourself, if you are imagining this through) and that you usually cannot afford to reach all of them, all of the time. These two composite considerations—within an individual and across individuals—will enable the manager or media planner to select the correct reach pattern for the media plan.

Reach patterns are extremely important to understand and identify. They are one of the two keys, along with effective frequency, to advanced media strategy.

CHAPTER 3

EFFECTIVE FREQUENCY

Having decided on the reach pattern, the second major component of media strategy is the estimation of effective frequency levels for the individual who are reached during the advertising cycles.

The concept of *effective frequency* asserts that an individual prospective customer has to be exposed to a brand's advertising a certain minimum number of times, within an advertising cycle, in order for the advertising to dispose the individual toward purchasing that brand (Longman 1971; Achenbaum 1977; Naples 1979). Effective frequency can consist of a *range* of exposures between the minimum effective frequency level and a possible maximum effective frequency level. Exposures within this range raise to a practical maximum the individual's *disposition* to purchase (probability of purchasing) the brand. Note that "purchase disposition" may be manifest as a store visit or purchase inquiry as far as advertising is concerned for some types of products and services (particularly high purchase-risk ones). The effective frequency concept is also applicable to on-going *promotion* campaigns for the brand.

This chapter explains effective frequency and shows how to estimate it. (The next chapter takes a more dynamic view of effective frequency and relates it to effective reach and active effective reach.) Frequency begins with the input and output concepts of insertions, exposures, and disposition to purchase. Next come the derivative concepts of minimum effective frequency and maximum effective frequency. A formula is provided for estimating minimum effective frequency per advertising cycle. The chapter concludes by showing how to adjust the estimate for non-standard ad units when these are used in the media plan.

3.1. Input and Output Concepts

Insertions of the ad or ads in the media schedule produce exposures, which may or may not affect individuals' dispositions to purchase. These input and output concepts are explained first.

3.1.1. INSERTIONS AND EXPOSURES

An *insertion* is the placement of an ad in a media vehicle. A media "schedule" comprises all the insertions that are placed in all the media vehicles used in the plan.

However (and here's the problem with media schedules shown only as shaded boxes on graph paper—the typical way in which managers see them): there is no necessary relationship between insertions in a media schedule and exposures that result from it.

- Insertions are the gross or aggregate input
- Exposures are the individual-level result

The varying relationship between insertions and exposures is easily understood with an example. Suppose an ad is inserted 4 times in a media schedule. If the 4 insertions are in the *same* media vehicle, it is quite likely that everyone reached by the vehicle will get 4 exposures to the ad. However, if the 4 insertions are in *different* media vehicles, hardly anyone will get 4 exposures—most of the individuals reached will get only 1 exposure. There have been 4 insertions in both cases, but the exposures to individuals that these insertions produce are very different. Insertions go in, and a *distribution* of exposures across individuals comes out. The distribution differs depending on the media vehicles in which the insertions are placed.

Effective frequency is based on *exposures*. "Exposure" means *placement of the advertisement in a media vehicle* that the target audience is *known or expected to see, hear or read*. The British term for exposures, OTS, or opportunities to see (or hear or read) the advertisement, nicely expresses what is meant by exposure.

OTS is an *opportunity* for exposure, not an actual exposure in the everyday sense of the word "exposure." Whether target audience individuals do in fact see, hear, or read the advertisement—that is, in Rossiter and Percy's (1987, 1997) terminology, whether they begin to *process* the advertisement by at least paying initial *attention* to it—is a function of: (1) the attention-getting characteristics of the media vehicle; (2) the size (time or space) of the advertising unit; and (3) the creative content of the advertisement.

The media planner must allow, up front, for (1) and (2), and how these allowances are made is explained in this chapter. If the creative "strength" of the ad or ads is known beforehand, notably from pre-test results, then (3) can be allowed for, too, but more typically the strength of the creative is not known until after the campaign has commenced, and adjustments to frequency of exposures are made then.

3.1.2. DISPOSITION TO PURCHASE

The final output component of the effective frequency concept requires clarification: this is the notion of "influencing" the next purchase. Whereas any degree of processing that occurs on any of the five communication effects (see Rossiter and Percy 1987, 1997) can be said to influence purchase to some extent, the media planner's focus should be on *disposition to purchase* and the role of effective frequency in raising this disposition to actionable threshold. *Threshold* is the level of stimulation (in this case the level of disposition) below which there is no action (purchase or purchase-related action). It is the minimum level of stimulation for action to occur.

Disposition to purchase (or for the target audience to take other, purchase-related action such as a store visit or an inquiry) is measured by the individual's "mental state" with regard to two of the communication effects, that jointly have to be present:

- *Brand awareness* (a necessary prerequisite to purchase) *plus*
- *Brand attitude* for low risk/transformational advertising, *or*
- *Brand purchase intention* for the other three types of advertising, namely, low risk/informational, high risk/informational and high risk/transformational advertising.

Brand awareness is obviously necessary for brand choice but the attitude or intention that must follow is different, depending on the type of brand choice. For low risk/transformational brand choice, a favorable brand attitude is sufficient. For the other three types, a more definite brand purchase intention (beyond attitude) is usually required (see Rossiter and Percy, 1997, chapters 5 and 19).

Those familiar with quantitative models of brand choice will see that "disposition" is equivalent to the individual's brand-purchase *probability*. This probability is brand preference (attitude or intention) *conditional* on brand *awareness* at the time of choice (cf. Urban and Hauser 1993, chapter 16). For this conditional probability to be "at threshold," it has to be higher than the conditional probability of purchasing any other competing brand, or at least equal to the probability of purchasing in the product category, if this is the only brand.

3.2. Minimum and Maximum Effective Frequency

3.2.1. MINIMUM EFFECTIVE FREQUENCY (MEF/c)

The manager or media planner's interest is primarily in estimate the *minimum* effective frequency necessary to raise purchase disposition to action threshold (see Figure 3.1). The minimum is sought because this is the frequency at which threshold disposition to purchase will be achieved at lowest cost.

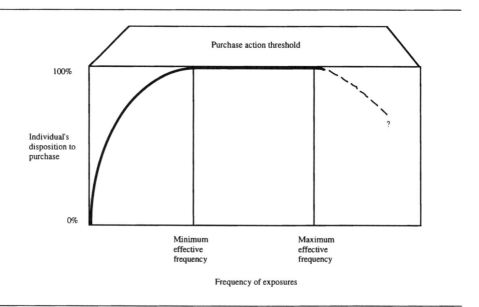

Figure 3.1. Individual threshold of disposition to purchase as a function of frequency of exposures.

The smallest minimum effective frequency necessary to cause disposition to purchase to be at threshold would be 1 exposure in the advertising cycle. This may be sufficient frequency for direct-response advertising, such as a direct mail offer—or with a promotion offer—where the target audience only has a chance to go through the buyer response sequence of exposure-to-action once. Also, as will be seen in the MEF/c formula, 1 exposure may be sufficient for an audience that is loyal to your brand. With word-of-mouth or personal influence, the required MEF could even be reduced to 0, though only temporarily.

In most advertising situations, however, the minimum effective frequency per advertising cycle will be greater than 1. Target audiences other than the brand's own loyal customers will increase the required MEF/c by 2 or 3 exposures, or more if the target is new category users. The nature of the brand's communication objectives or the presence of competing brands' communication effects also will increase the required MEF to a number above 1 exposure.

The MEF/c estimation formula, the focus of Section 3.3, will examine the factors that determine minimum effective frequency, and show how to estimate minimum effective frequency for any advertising situation. From now on, minimum effective frequency will be abbreviated as MEF. Also, to emphasize that MEF must always be considered over a fixed time interval, namely MEF per advertising cycle, the form k/c or k+/c will be used, where k is the number of exposures (MEF value) and c is the duration of the advertising cycle.

3.2.2. MAXIMUM EFFECTIVE FREQUENCY (MaxEF/c)

Disposition to purchase becomes a horizontal line when exposure frequency goes beyond the minimum effective frequency needed for purchase (see Figure 3.1 earlier) and in some situations could turn downward (the dotted line in the figure). For cost reasons, and because of the downturn possibility, the manager or media planner may wish to specify a *maximum* effective frequency per cycle, or MaxEF/c.

The setting of a number for maximum effective frequency per ad cycle (MaxEF/c) is more complex than it first appears, however. Three different situations can be distinguished: non-carryover reach patterns, reach patterns *with* carryover, and the possibility of ad "wearout."

When the advertising is supposed to work only during its advertising cycle (non-carryover), it is clear that the MaxEF/c is *the same as MEF/c*. Exposures beyond MEF/c are a waste of money when the prospect is already "sold" (direct-response campaigns are probably the obvious example of this; see Section 3.3.3). Non-carryover reach patterns, where the advertiser should aim for MEF/c *and not much more*, are: blitz and short-term fad (new products) and shifting reach (established products). It may help here to briefly look back at Chapter 2's reach pattern diagrams.

Reach patterns *with* carryover, however, have a very different interpretation of exposures beyond MEF/c. These reach patterns are: wedge and reverse-wedge/PI (new products), and regular purchase cycle, awareness, and seasonal priming (established products). All require that the advertising's effects last beyond the actual cycle, c, and hopefully through every hiatus between successive cycles. Here, "excessive" exposures beyond MEF/c are actually the main cause of carryover. You therefore have to set a *new, higher value* of MEF/c to achieve carryover. The new value of MEF, in an ad cycle, will then depend on how long a duration you want the *original MEF level* to carry over for. (This decision is discussed at length in Chapter 4.) Whether there is a *MaxEF* to be considered is then entirely due to the next situation.

The final situation in MaxEF/c consideration is for ads that can "wear out" if repeated too often or too close together. (Note that this could occur either in a non-carryover or a carryover reach pattern. That is, it is a *possible* extension of the first and second situations.) In broadcast media (TV and radio), there is the risk that purchase disposition can turn downwards (see the dotted line in Figure 3.1 earlier), especially for transformational ads receiving excessive "captive" exposures. In print media (newspapers, magazines, outdoor and posters, direct mail) and in the print-like medium of Internet websites, the problem is much more likely to be loss of attention, which won't decrease disposition but won't contribute to it either. The only solution in all cases is to attempt to find the *individual ad's* MaxEF/c and to introduce a new execution, or executions, at that number. An individual ad's MaxEF/c is highly variable for broadcast ads and no theoretical guide can be given; direct inspection of tracking survey results has to be used. For print media, Brown (1994) provides evidence that 3 OTS is the typical MaxEF/c before attention loss becomes substantial, although again of course there are occasional exceptions.

To reiterate, MaxEF/c determination depends on the situation: if carryover is not needed, then MaxEF/c is theoretically the same as MEF/c but, to be practical, since frequency achieved in media schedules may be a bit optimistic as the exposures are just opportunities to see, hear or read the ad, set MaxEF/c at 1 or 2 exposures beyond MEF/c; if carryover is needed, then a higher, "carryover" MEF/c is used and MaxEF/c depends only on the next situation; which is that if individual ads are anticipated to wear out quickly if repeated too often or too closely within a cycle in either a non-carryover or a carryover reach pattern, then it's the individual ad's MaxEF/c that you need to measure so that you can introduce a new execution or executions of the ad.

3.2.3. AVERAGE FREQUENCY IS UNINFORMATIVE

Media planners conventionally describe media plans in terms of the average frequency delivered (among those individuals who are reached) in a particular time period. Average frequency is uninformative. Indeed, McDonald (1996a) calls the average frequency statistics that appear in conventional media plans "strictly meaningless abstracts" (p. 134). This can be illustrated easily with a set of diagrams (Figure 3.2) showing hypothetical *frequency distributions* for alternative media plans. All have an average frequency of exactly 2 (total exposures divided by reach equals average frequency). But in terms of effective reach, if the MEF is 1, then plans A and B are best; if MEF equals 2, then Plan A is best; if MEF equals 3, Plan B is best; if MEF equals 4, Plan C is best; and if MEF equals 5, Plan D is best. Obviously, average frequency tells us next to nothing about a media plan's effectiveness.

A serious delusion for marketing managers, and media planners, is due to the fact that most frequency distributions (exposure distributions) are right-skewed (peak to the *left*, or low-frequency end, and tail to the right, or high-frequency end, like Plan D in the figure). This being so, the average frequency will almost always exaggerate the frequency at which the *typical* target audience individual is reached. The typical person gets the *mode*, and the mode of a right-skewed distribution is always less than the mean.

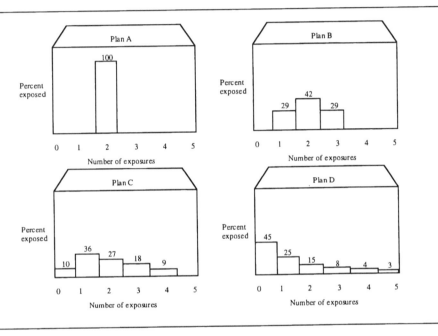

Figure 3.2. Hypothetical frequency distributions of exposures, all with average frequency = 2. Now compare them for increasing levels of MEF.

A manager informed that a plan is delivering an average frequency of 2 exposures per week is likely to think that at least half the individuals reached (the "average") are receiving 2 exposures when in reality it is far fewer than half, depending on the degree of skew. Average frequency is a statistic best forgotten.

Average frequency, therefore, must be replaced by the estimation and reporting of effective frequency. Effective frequency is the only type of frequency that matters, and it is an *individual-level exposures* phenomenon.

3.3. Estimating Minimum Effective Frequency

Estimating the *minimum* effective frequency will be the focus of this section of the chapter. The question of the *maximum* effective frequency level, beyond which exposures are either a waste of budget or, for an individual ad, negatively effective, was answered in the previous section.

3.3.1. MEF/c ESTIMATION FORMULA

The minimum effective frequency per advertising cycle (MEF/c) has to be estimated before the media plan can be finalized. Only in the case of an established brand that has been tracked over many years will the manager have a good idea of what the MEF is, and then only if the market hasn't changed. Another expensive and time-consuming option would be to try different frequency levels in test markets, but few advertisers can afford this. In most cases, meaning the great majority, MEF/c will have to be *estimated*.

What can be stated at the outset is that no single number for MEF can possibly be correct for all circumstances, and certainly not without a time period, c, specified. This rules out the use of simplistic, single-number solutions such as "3-hit" theory or "3+" (Naples 1979), which is still popular today, and usually without a time limit for the 3 exposures specified, and more recently "single-exposure" theory or "1/week" (Ephron 1995; Jones 1995, though rather major exceptions are made by Jones 1997). Only in very particular circumstances could either of these particular numbers be right, and the time period *must* be specified. The empirical evidence against there being any one "magic number" for MEF/c is overwhelming (Zielske 1986; Broadbent 1996; McDonald 1996a, 1996b, 1996c; Roberts 1996; Cowling 1997). These investigators show that there are wide variations in the number of exposures per time period that will cause sales for different brands to peak. This is as expected, but the knowledge that there will be an empirical right number (or rate) to be found for the campaign in the marketplace does not, as noted, help the manager who must make an estimate before the campaign starts in order to buy the media schedule. A rational *a priori* approach is needed.

The present approach to minimum effective frequency estimation, to provide an MEF/c formula, makes use of the theory and findings in Rossiter and Percy (1997) relating to target audiences and communication objectives. The formula assumes that 1 exposure in the advertising cycle (1/c) is the beginning or "building block" level, then adds and in one situation subtracts exposures according to four factors (actually five, as the third has two factors in it): vehicle attention (VA), target audience (TA), communication objectives (namely brand awareness, BA, and brand attitude, BATT), and personal influence (PI).

The formula is MEF/c = 1 + VA × (TA + BA + BATT + PI). The values for VA, etc., are given in Table 3.1. The factors are briefly explained below (for more detail, see Rossiter and Percy 1997, chapter 16) and then the use of the formula is illustrated.

Vehicle Attention (VA). Media vehicles differ in the level of attention given them by the typical audience member. Vehicle attention constrains exposure, that is, it places limits on the *opportunity* for the ad to achieve attention. There have been many studies of attention to various media types and media vehicles using observational methods or, more often, self-report measures (see Rossiter and Percy 1997, chapter 16, for details of these). The practical outcome of these studies is that the media planner can achieve a reasonably accurate frequency weighting factor by dividing media vehicles into just two classes: high attention vehicles and low attention vehicles.

For *high* attention vehicles—prime-time TV and daytime serials, primary-reader newspapers, primary-reader magazines, radio just prior to headline news and weather bulletins, *stationary* outdoor and posters, direct mail, and websites—the effective frequency stays at 1 exposure (prior to the other three correction factors being applied).

For *low* attention vehicles—all other TV day parts, regular-listening day parts on radio, passalong-reader newspapers, passalong-reader magazines and *mobile* outdoor and posters—the effective frequency should be *doubled* (doubling the effective frequency calculated from the remaining three correction factors). The reason for the doubled frequency is that the individual's probability of attention to these media vehicles is about half that of high attention vehicles, so that double the frequency is needed to give the ad an equal chance of being attended to.

TABLE 3.1. Minimum effective frequency (MEF/c) estimation factors and their numerical correction values. The formula is MEF/c = 1 + VA × (TA + BA + BATT + PI).

FACTOR	−1	0	+1	+2	LC + 1*
		CORRECTION (STARTING FROM 1 EXPOSURE IN ADVERTISING CYCLE)			
1. Vehicle attention			high attention	low attention	
2. Target audience		brand loyals	brand switchers	other-brand switchers, other-brand loyals	new category users
3. Communication objectives (two factors)		brand recognition			brand recall
		informational brand attitude			transform-ational brand attitude
4. Personal influence	high (average contact ≥ .25)	low (average contact < .25)			

* If market share leader, use +2 exposures; if not leader, set equal to largest competitor's average frequency +1 (called LC + 1). LC + 1 is additive on the 1 only; for example, a campaign aimed at new category users, with brand recall and transformational brand attitude objectives, would use LC + 3 exposures.

Target Audience (TA). Some target audiences have more to learn about the brand than other target audiences. Brand loyals (BLs) have little or nothing extra to learn, so no exposures need to be added for advertising to this audience. Favorable brand switchers (FBSs) seem to need at least 2 exposures in the advertising cycle (2/c) before switching is induced (McDonald 1971; Gullen and Johnson 1986; both studies being based on 2-week advertising cycles), so 1 more exposure is added to the building block level of 1 exposure. Other-brand switchers (OBSs) and other-brand loyals (OBLs), assuming that a message strategy has been found that promises to be effective with these typically more negative target audiences, such as refutational advertising or comparative advertising, have some new learning to undergo, so 2 more exposures are added (3/c total) when advertising to this group.

New category users (NCUs) require the most new learning because they have to learn about the category as well as the advertised brand. Most NCU target audience situations will occur with new brands early in the product category life cycle in a growing market, where market share, not simply sales, is the major objective. Peckham (1981) and later Schroer (1990) have demonstrated that the only way to increase market share (assuming equivalent creative effectiveness) is to advertise more than the *leading competitor (LC)*. This means trying to reach more potential new category users than competitors are reaching (greater penetration) and reaching each potential user with higher frequency than the leading competitor.

To out-advertise the largest competitor, you will need to estimate the *largest competitor's MEF*; this can be done by running the largest competitor through the MEF/c formula, using +2 instead of LC (see below) and remembering to nominate the competitor's target audience. You then need to exceed this frequency by at least 1 exposure (called LC + 1) per advertising cycle, therefore producing (LC + 1)/c. Exceeding the largest competitor's overall frequency by more than 1 would be even better, remembering that it is almost impossible to over-advertise a new brand or to a new-user target. However, a margin of 1 exposure per cycle should be sufficient frequency to wage an effective market share battle if the advertising message is comparably good. Of course, there is some chance of the LC's frequency escalating if the largest competitor realizes what you are doing and decides to respond. This appears to happen sometimes when new soft drinks or new beer brands are launched, both heavily-advertised categories. There is no way to avoid this escalation except by finding brilliant creative that works with fewer exposures.

Of course, your brand may *be* the largest brand that is targeting NCUs. If so, you have to set effective frequency according to the other factors, since there is no larger competitor to overtake. The recommendation is +2 exposures above the building block level (equal to that for OBSs and OBLs) because the amount of new learning, even for a monopolizing brand, is substantial. The emergence of a fast-gaining competitor using heavy advertising would, however, indicate a change to a defensive posture by you as the leading brand and use of LC + 1 *as if* the fast-gaining brand were the largest competitor.

Communication Objectives (BA and BATT). The foregoing target audience correction factor already has allowed for the initial level of communication effects within target audience individuals by using a higher frequency when the effects are at or near zero (new category users) down to no adjustment when the effects are at or near a maximum (brand loyals). However, further adjustments are necessary depending on particular communication objectives.

The two communication objectives requiring the biggest differences in effective frequency are brand awareness (BA) and brand attitude (BATT). The reasoning underlying the brand awareness and brand attitude adjustments is presented in detail in Rossiter and Percy (1997, chapters 8 and 9) can be summarized as follows.

The first factor is the type of brand awareness. If brand *recognition* is the objective, no additional frequency will be needed so no extra exposures are added (subject, of course, to the other correction factors and notably introductory advertising to NCUs). In contrast, if brand *recall* is the objective, the frequency needed will be relatively high—with an emphasis on the "relative." It is virtually impossible to make the frequency for brand recall too high (see studies by Singh and Rothschild 1983, and Schultz and Block 1986). The maximum level for brand recall would be everyone in the target audience recalling the brand first, which happens for only a very few heavily advertised brands. Therefore, LC + 1 is recommended for brand recall; that is, set the effective frequency level at least 1 exposure higher than the estimated MEF/c used by the *largest competitor*, or use +2 if your brand already *is* the largest competitor in the category.

Brand attitude strategy (Rossiter and Percy 1997, chapters 8 and 9) is the other communication factor that affects effective frequency in the media plan. The involvement or brand purchase risk component of brand attitude strategy already is allowed for in the target audience correction factor, whereby purchase risk increases as the audience is changed from brand loyals to new category users; to correct again would be redundant. However, a correction is applied for the purchase motivation component. An *informational* brand attitude strategy should be effective within the first 1 or 2 exposures—the brand is perceived immediately as either solving a problem or as irrelevant. Hence no adjustment is recommended for informational advertising. A transformational brand attitude strategy, by contrast, requires heavy repetition—for build-up *and* for reinforcement of the brand image or attitude. The LC + 1 adjustment is recommended for transformational advertising.

The brand awareness and brand attitude correction factors for effective frequency are combined by addition. A brand recognition/informational attitude campaign would require no additional frequency (subject again to the other correction factors). A brand recognition/transformational attitude campaign, or a brand recall/informational attitude campaign, would require +2 or LC + 1 exposures. And, highest of all, a brand recall/transformational attitude campaign would require +4 or LC + 2 exposures (note that only the +1's are added when adding LC + 1's). Beer and fast-food restaurants would be two examples of categories that would use brand recall/transformational attitude campaigns and these categories are among the nation's most frequent advertisers.

Personal Influence (PI). The last of the correction factors for estimating minimum effective frequency per advertising cycle is personal influence (PI). Personal influence refers to social diffusion of the advertising message, usually via word of mouth but alternatively or additionally by visual influence, as when brands are seen by others in a reference group or reference individual context. PI was assumed in the reverse-wedge reach pattern in Chapter 2. Now it is explicitly incorporated in terms of frequency.

Personal influence, providing it is favorable (which the advertiser would check during the advertising strategy and ad testing stages of research and then double-check during campaign tracking once the campaign is launched), has a number of advantages over advertising *per se*. First, it is free, which means that the advertiser saves on advertising costs. Second, 1 word-of-mouth contact appears to be about twice as effective as 1 advertising exposure (Herr, Kardes and Kim 1991), probably because a favorable brand attitude or advertising *attitude* is nearly always conveyed rather than just awareness (Sheth 1971; Day 1971). Third, personal influence can operate at any stage of the life cycle for any type of product, not just new, high-risk products as was commonly believed (Holmes and Lett 1977). In particular, a new *advertising* campaign, even for an old brand, can trigger word of mouth.

Ozga (1960) proposed that social diffusion serves as a substitute for part of the total amount of advertising that would otherwise be required. He introduced the notion of a *contact coefficient*, based on the average number of other people told about the advertising by the average individual exposed to it (this could of course be extended to include visual contact). From Rossiter and Percy's (1987) synthesis of the available studies of interpersonal influence, it is estimated that a contact coefficient of at least .25 is necessary to justify reducing the effective frequency estimate by 1 exposure. This means that for every 4 people reached by the advertising, at least 1 person contacts at least 1 other person during the advertising cycle. Because this contact should be doubly effective, and because it may spread, it in effect replaces an exposure. Thus, a contact coefficient of at least .25 seems a reasonable figure to justify a reduction of 1 exposure (that is, −1) in the minimum effective frequency calculation. For a personal contact coefficient of less than .25, no adjustment is made.

Some examples—while the ads were new—might be Benetton's "United Colors" ads (outside the U.S.A. because the most controversial ads were not used there); Nike's "Just do it" ads; and Coke's much-loved "Polar bears and seal" ad. Hard-hitting industrial comparative ads may sometimes reach the −1 value for PI, such as Hewlett-Packard's 1998 attack on Digital computers, questioning Digital's commitment to the Unix operating system after Digital merged with Compaq.

With personal influence, there should be no reduction in the *reach* of the media plan. This is because personal influence works best when the "other" person contacted has also seen the campaign (discussing an ad with someone who has not seen it is somewhat frustrating, whereas discussing it with someone who has seen it is usually mutually reinforcing). The media strategy is to maintain the reach while reducing the required number of exposures because of the bonus exposure created by interpersonal influence.

Examples of MEF/c Calculations

Several examples will illustrate how the MEF/c formula can be applied. The very lowest effective frequency would be no advertising (0 exposures) in the advertising cycle. However, this would only occur in one particular circumstance, and not indefinitely but rather between flights. This circumstance would be following a high-attention vehicle campaign (for example, prime-time TV), aimed at brand loyals, for a brand purchased via brand recognition, and sold via an informational brand attitude strategy—which also generated strong personal influence. It would be quite rare for a campaign to meet all these criteria simultaneously. Campaigns likely to generate strong word-of-mouth would be new campaigns rather than campaigns directed with low frequency at brand loyals.

Most estimates of minimum effective frequency will be between 1 and 13 exposures per advertising cycle. Some hypothetical examples of MEFs calculated from the formula are as follows (for simplicity, a *regular purchase cycle* reach pattern is assumed, that is, the length of an advertising cycle = c = one purchase cycle, in weeks). The numbers in parentheses are the numerical values to be plugged into the formula MEF/c = 1 + VA × (TA + BA + BATT + PI).

- Miller beer (1+), advertising in primary-reader magazines (VA = 1 ×), to brand switchers (TA = 1), via a brand recognition (BA = 0), and a taste-based transformational brand attitude strategy (oversimplifying here from the correct procedure given shortly: for BATT = LC + 1, assume Budweiser, the largest competitor, is using +2 and then add 1), with no personal influence (PI = 0) = 1 + 1 × [1 + 0 + (2 + 1) + 0] = 5 exposures per purchase cycle, which is probably about two weeks for beer. Thus 5/2.
- Tide detergent (1+), advertising on daytime TV serials (VA = 1 ×), to other-brand loyals (TA = 2), via a brand recognition (BA = 0) and informational brand attitude strategy (BATT = 0), with no personal influence (PI = 0) = 1 + 1 × (2 + 0 + 0 + 0) = 3 exposures per purchase cycle, which is probably about three weeks for detergent. Thus 3/3.
- Radio Shack (1+), advertising on radio (double the following, that is, VA = 2 ×), to new category users, as the market leader (TA = 2), via a brand recall (BA = 2) and informational brand attitude strategy (BATT = 0) with no personal influence (PI = 0) = 1 + 2 × (2 + 2 + 0 + 0) = 9 exposures per purchase cycle, which is probably about 10-weekly for this type of retailer. Thus 9/10.

Theoretically, the highest MEF would occur with a late entry trying to break into a new category, with communication objectives that require brand recall and a transformational brand attitude, by using a low-attention medium, such as radio, passalong-reader newspapers or magazines, or daytime TV other than serials. Such media normally would not be chosen for a new product campaign, but if they were, it can be seen that an MEF of at least 13 exposures per advertising cycle would be needed. For frequently-purchased consumer products, this would be a very expensive campaign.

However, for consumer durables or industrial products, this would be feasible because of the longer purchase cycle, with the budget spread by using either the awareness reach pattern or the shifting reach pattern explained in Chapter 2.

MEF for the Largest Competitor (LC)

The MEF for the largest competitor, required when LC occurs in the formula, can be *approximated* by running the largest competitor through the formula, using +2 to reflect market leader status. Then substitute the LC value in the formula and calculate your own MEF. For example, consider 7UP against Coke, assuming a high attention vehicle, brand recognition, and a transformational brand attitude strategy. Coke would probably be using MEF/c = 1 + 1(0 + 0 + 2 + 0) = 3/c for its BLs. For 7UP, this target audience would be OBLs, and 7UP's MEF/c would be 1 + 1[+ 2 + 0 + (3 + 1) + 0] = 7/c. Note that Coke's 3 exposures are substituted for the LC term in 7UP's MEF calculation.

LC in Low Attention Vehicles

There is a caution when using the MEF formula and LC occurs with a low attention vehicle (VA = 2). In this case, you must correct VA = 2 back to VA = 1. The reason is that the largest competitor presumably has *already* doubled its frequency to reflect the low attention vehicle, so you don't want to "double double."

MEF Across High and Low Attention Vehicles
Media plans may be based on a mixture of high and low attention media vehicles—such as prime-time TV (high) and early-morning daytime TV (low); or newspapers (high) plus radio (low). In these situations, it is best to: (1) calculate the MEF gross as if for all high attention, (2) estimate how many of the MEF exposures are likely to be contributed by the low attention vehicles, (3) then double *that* number and add it to the net high attention number obtained by subtraction in the second step. For example, suppose the high-attention MEF is 6, and that prime-time TV ads are expected to contribute 4 and ads on regular-listening radio 2. Set the MEF *for TV* at 4, and the MEF *for radio* at 2 × 2 = 4. There are the *respective* MEFs to aim for *when* using the two media together. Although an MEF/c of 8/c is produced, it is equivalent to an MEF/c of 6/c if only high attention vehicles were used.

3.3.2. AD UNIT ADJUSTMENTS TO MEF/c

Throughout the applications of the MEF/c formula, it has been assumed that the advertiser is using *standard* ad units—that is, 30-second broadcast commercials, 1-page print ads, and so forth. However, some campaigns, especially those introducing new products or services, consist mostly or entirely of longer commercials or larger print ads. To the opposite extreme, campaigns for familiar products and services may employ many shorter or smaller ads, usually in an effort to increase frequency (and often individual continuity) for the same expenditure. Clearly, *non-standard* ad units do not make the same contribution as standard units to achieving MEF/c. Longer or larger ads, or color ads in a mainly black & white ad environment, have more opportunity to achieve the communication effects leading to disposition. Shorter or smaller ads have less opportunity. It follows that the original MEF/c estimate should be *reduced* if longer (etc.) ads are to be used predominantly in the cycle, and *increased* if shorter (etc.) ads are to be used.

It would be relatively easy to calculate the ad-unit adjusted MEF/c if ad units had simple proportional effects on attention (attention is the response used to provide the ad unit adjustment values). However, doubling length or size, for instance, doesn't mean exactly double the attention or contribution to MEF, and halving the length or size doesn't exactly make half the contribution. The main adjustment values for mass media ad units are shown in Table 3.2. More detailed tables are available in Rossiter and Percy (1997, chapter 10) but the summary table here is sufficient for most media plan applications.

The MEF/c estimate itself is adjusted by *dividing* the original estimate by the ad-unit adjustment value. For instance, if the original MEF estimate is 4, and 4-color newspaper ad units are used (a value of 1.8 in the table), the adjusted MEF is 4 / 1.8 = 2.2. To be safe, and because MEF must be a whole-number frequency, this number is rounded *up*. Thus MEF = 3. That is, a received frequency of three 4-color ads is expected to produce the same disposition as four black & white ads (all 1-page newspaper ads). On the other hand, if half-page black & white ads were used (a value of 0.7 in the table), the adjusted MEF is 4 / 0.7 = 5.7, or 6 rounded up. Exposure to six smaller-ad insertions would be needed to produce the same disposition as four 1-page standard ads.

TABLE 3.2. Ad unit adjustments (contributions to MEF/c) for mass media ads

Commercial length	Television		Radio	
:60	1.2		1.4	
:30 (standard)	1.0		1.0	
:15	.8		.8	
:10	.7		.7	
Print ad size	Newspapers	Consumer magazines	Industrial magazines
2-page spread	1.2	1.3	1.7
1 page (standard)	1.0	1.0	1.0
½ page	.7	.7	.7
¼ page	.5	.4	.4
Print ad color	Newspapers	Consumer magazines	Industrial magazines
4-color	1.8	1.0 (std)	1.4
2-color	1.5	.8	1.2
Black & white	1.0 (std)	.7	1.0 (std)
Location		Outdoor and poster	
Competitive (standard)		1.0	
Stand-alone		2.5	

One thing to note with print ads is that when the two ad-unit factors of size and color are used in the one ad, the adjustment values multiply (for instance, a 2-page, 4-color newspaper ad contributes $1.2 \times 1.8 = 2.2$ to MEF; a quarter-page, 2-color industrial magazine ad contributes $0.4 \times 1.2 = 0.5$ to MEF). As before, the resulting value is divided into the original MEF value to obtain the ad-unit adjusted MEF/c.

Detailed tables of non-standard ad-unit adjustments for all media are provided in Rossiter and Percy (1997, chapter 10) and are worth consulting by advertisers who often employ non-standard ad units in their campaigns.

3.3.3. MEF/c AND MaxEF/c FOR DIRECT-RESPONSE ADS AND PROMOTIONS

Common sense suggests that one "good opportunity" to see, read or hear it should be sufficient for a direct-response ad or an advertised promotion offer. In fact, it can be assumed that a *point-of-purchase* promotion offer gets only one opportunity to work (MEF/c *and* MaxEF/c = 1). In general, however, whether the first "good opportunity" occurs at OTS = 1 will depend on the medium in which the DR ad or offer appears and also on the communication-effects status of the target audience.

DR media that allow plenty of opportunity to process the ad or offer on the 1st OTS include: TV infomercials (because they are long and almost always repeat the main selling points) and nearly all types of "print" media, notably websites, direct mail, newspapers, magazines, and stationary outdoor and posters—though not mobile outdoor and posters—because these media allow the respondent to process the ad or offer "ad lib." In contrast, television and radio DR ads, excluding infomercials, allow only 30 to 90 seconds, typically, before the ad or offer is "gone," which implies that 2 or 3 OTS would be needed for broadcast DR ads to provide a sufficient "good opportunity."

Survey evidence indicates that even in high-opportunity-to-process DR media, only about 1 in 4 people respond (inquire or purchase) on the 1st OTS. For instance, across all infomercials on U.S. cable TV (National Infomercial Marketing Association 1994), it was found that 27 percent of total respondents acted after 1 OTS, 31 percent after 2, 18 percent after 3, 9 percent after 4 (the cumulative response is now 85 percent), and the remaining 15 percent required 5 or more OTS. Similarly, in another high-opportunity-to-process medium, industrial magazines, Fox, Reddy and Rao (1997) found that in one DR campaign, 32 percent of those who responded did so on the first insertion (which would be the 1st OTS for those reached) and 85 percent, cumulatively, had responded after the third insertion (which may have been only the 1st or 2nd rather than the 3rd *OTS*, given the somewhat uneven readership of industrial magazines); and in a second campaign, the figures were 18 percent on the first insertion and 85 percent, cumulatively, after the fourth insertion. These distributions of responses, in both the infomercial and industrial magazine examples, imply purchase disposition differences within the overall audience reached. The "instant responders," about one-quarter of the total, may have had a very strong category need and sized up the offer sufficiently in 1 OTS to decide that the offer would meet that need. The "other respondents," about three-quarters of the total, despite the high opportunity to process the 1st exposure, seemed to require 2 to 4 exposures before the communication effects of the DR ad attained a sufficient threshold to convince them to inquire or buy.

With the relatively more difficult-to-process DR media, namely television and radio, at least 2 OTS would seem to be necessary for most potential respondents to comprehend the message. For DR TV, Danaher and Green (1997) studied 12 campaigns which used, respectively, DR commercials of 30-second to 90-second lengths (not infomercials). Although the study did not report the response per OTS, it is noteworthy that the typical campaign was run for an *average* frequency of just 3 OTS, which would imply a peak response at about 2 OTS and a cumulative majority response by about 4 OTS. No studies could be found for radio DR ads, but the normally lower attention paid to radio suggests that about 3 to 5 OTS may be the effective range.

Putting the theoretical considerations and limited evidence together, the following MEF/c and MaxEF/c guidelines are suggested. MaxEF/c is important for DR campaigns because the advertiser does not want to continue running the ad after most of the response has been exhausted (see Danaher and Green 1997 for a discussion of response incidence, which is the relevant criterion for high-margin items, and cost per response, which is the relevant criterion for low-margin items). The guidelines are shown in Table 3.3.

DR ads are often over-length or over-size ad units, such as 60-second TV or radio commercials or much longer infomercials, or 2-page or multi-page print ads or brochures. Theoretically, these non-standard ad units contribute more than 1.0 to MEF, as indicated in Table 3.2 earlier, which would reduce the required MEF (and MaxEF).

However, it seems safer to stay closer to the empirical evidence and ignore ad-unit adjustments for DR ads, using the guidelines presented in Table 3.3.

TABLE 3.3. Recommended MEF/c and MaxEF/c for direct-response ads and promotions

Medium/ad type	MEF/c	MaxEF/c
Cable TV or radio infomercials; television using :30 to :120 ads; newspapers; magazines; stationary outdoor and posters; direct mail; websites	2	4
Radio using :30 to :120 ads	3	5
Point-of-purchase promotions	1	1

Conclusions About Effective Frequency Estimation
It can be seen that the estimation of effective frequency is not easy, which perhaps explains why many media planners fall back on simplistic rules of thumb. However, this is your *budget* that is involved here. Unnecessary extra frequency wastes money, and it is well worth noting that additional frequency will not improve the sales results of an ad that is not persuasive to begin with (Adams and Blair 1992). On the other hand, under-frequency wastes the budget too by not giving the ad or ads an adequate opportunity to work.

Effective frequency is therefore worth considerable effort to estimate accurately. It commits the budget expenditure for the first part of the campaign until the frequency level can be determined accurately through campaign tracking research. And there's more to be decided for campaigns that rely on advertising carryover or on tactical adjustments to frequency, or both. These decisions are covered in the next chapter.

CHAPTER 4

CARRYOVER AND OTHER FREQUENCY DECISIONS

(Minimum) effective frequency is of course used in media planning to calculate the *effective reach* of the campaign, per advertising cycle. But many campaigns are designed to last beyond the time at which the ad or ads appear, that is, to "carry over." About the only approach to handling this has been Broadbent's (1979, 1984) concept of *Adstock* (also Broadbent and Fry 1995), which is based on GRPs. In this chapter, a more precise frequency-based approach is presented. It uses the notion that *attained* MEF/c is not a constant value, except in the short term. Changes in MEF/c requirements is the other remaining topic that completes a thorough examination of frequency decisions.

4.1. Effective Reach and Active Effective Reach

Having introduced the MEF/c estimation formula, there is one more important decision that has so far been deliberately ignored for simplicity's sake, and it concerns advertising *carryover*. This is incorporated, via MEF/c, by extending the concept of effective reach into what can be termed *active* effective reach.

Academics in marketing usually attempt to measure the carryover effects of advertising in terms of delayed (or "lagged") sales, that is, purchases that occur after the advertising flight or cycle, c, is over (see Leone 1995 for a review of these studies). However, as Givon and Horsky (1990) have pointed out, delayed sales are a confounded measure because these sales could be caused either by the persisting effects of the brand's advertising, representing advertising carryover, or by "purchase reinforcement" due to the presence or performance of the brand itself, among buyers of the brand. The package could continue to remind buyers of the brand, if it is a multiple-usage product such as coffee or washing powder (Priemer 1990), or the satisfactory performance of the product itself could reinforce repeat purchase by maintaining the communication effects —notably brand awareness and brand attitude—in the absence of advertising (Givon and Horsky 1990). Sorting out the relative contributions of true advertising carryover and purchase reinforcement is an almost impossible task; also, the latter would presumably vary for each brand depending on its "penetration," or proportion of buyers.

Practitioners, on the other hand, have tended to favor advertising "memory" or advertising awareness measures to estimate advertising carryover. Advertising awareness measures are not perfect, either, because it cannot be shown to be *necessary* that the brand's ad or ads have to be remembered in order for the advertising to have had an effect on the brand's communication effects of, say, brand awareness and brand attitude or brand purchase intention (or "disposition," to use the MEF criterion). People often retain messages while forgetting the source. However, advertising awareness at least has the advantage that it is less likely to be confounded by purchase reinforcement —which brand-based communication effects measures would undoubtedly be affected by, because these communication effects are increased by the "purchase reinforcement" purchases (not just purchase but also the communication effects are reinforced by satisfactory product performance). Advertising awareness therefore provides arguably the best practical measure of advertising carryover.

Using Advertising Awareness to Estimate Carryover

Perhaps the best-known measure of advertising awareness for estimating advertising carryover is Millward Brown's *brand-prompted claimed advertising recall* measure (Colman and Brown 1983; Millward Brown 1992). In this survey measure, respondents are shown a list of brands (hence brand-prompted) and asked which brands they (claim to) "have seen or heard advertised recently." The percentage of respondents claiming to have seen or heard advertising for the brand "recently" during the weeks when the brand has *not* advertised is the measure of advertising carryover. Carryover is represented by the perception that the brand is "still advertising" when it's not.

Millward Brown's researchers estimate that a constant carryover rate of 90 percent per week fits most campaigns well. As 90 percent of the advertising awareness carries over from week to week, the 2-week carryover would be $(.9 \times .9 =)$ 81 percent, the 3-week carryover $(.9^3 =)$ 73 percent, and the 4-week carryover $(.9^4 =)$ 66 percent. Obviously, highly memorable, brand-linked ads will carry over better, and less memorable *or* poorly brand-linked campaigns will have less carryover, by this measure. However, the "90 percent per week" carryover figure is a good up-front starting estimate prior to being able to track advertising awareness in the actual campaign.

To apply the carryover factor to the MEF/c estimate, a further assumption has to be made. Millward Brown's measure is an aggregate or "total sample" measure; thus, *of those respondents reached during the flight*, 90 percent of respondents claim to recall the brand being advertising when questioned 1 week after the flight, falling to 81 percent of respondents when questioned 2 weeks after, and so on. The assumption made now is that this carryover rate also applies at the *individual* level—that is, that the typical individual retains 90 percent of the frequency (MEF or higher) from the cycle a week after, then 81 percent 2 weeks after, and so on.

It should be evident that whereas advertising carryover can be very helpful in maintaining MEF between exposures, its opposite, the loss or "decay" of advertising effects, means loss of MEF, depending on the interval between exposures and the interval between cycles if there is more than one cycle in the overall media planning period. These intervals affect the estimates of effective reach and active effective reach, as discussed next.

4.1.1. EFFECTIVE REACH DURING THE ADVERTISING CYCLE

Effective reach was defined earlier (Chapter 1) as the number of target audience individuals reached at the effective frequency level (MEF or higher) in an advertising cycle. More microscopically, because ad insertions produce a distribution of exposures across individuals, some individuals will reach MEF relatively early in the cycle and others not until the end of the cycle, on the last OTS. Effective reach is measured as the cumulative number at MEF or higher at the *end* of the cycle. This is the figure that the manager is interested in, for instance, in "immediate" reach patterns that don't require carryover: blitz, short-term fad, and shifting reach (see Chapter 2).

As a rule of thumb, the MEF/c estimate should be fine as long as, for the great majority of individuals, the exposures in the cycle occur no longer than 1 week apart since, usually, there is no more than 10 percent loss of MEF. On the other hand, if the exposures are received *more than 1 week apart*, then allowance should be made using "over-frequency" as explained below for active effective reach. This could happen, for instance, in a campaign using monthly magazines. Even if several monthly magazines are used, the exposures are often likely to occur more than a week apart, and certainly if only one such magazine is used. To recap: if exposures during the cycle are no more than a week apart, the estimate of effective reach at the end of the cycle is regarded as accurate based on normal MEF/c.

4.1.2. ACTIVE EFFECTIVE REACH

Active effective reach was defined earlier (Chapter 1) as the number of target audience individuals who retain the effective frequency level for a given duration after the previous advertising cycle. (It can now be seen that it may be relevant also during an advertising cycle if the exposures are received more than a week apart. But, for discussion purposes, the post-cycle active effective reach will be assumed. The calculations are the same.)

One of the lesser-known findings of the early psychologist Ebbinghaus (1885), which, like most of his findings, has since been replicated many times (Mazur 1994), is the phenomenon of *overlearning*. This refers to the fact that additional repetitions beyond those sufficient for perfect immediate learning (cf. MEF) will improve performance on a *delayed* test (cf. the hiatus period up to the next cycle). Presumably, this is because the extra exposures help to offset the decay of effects that begins after the learning period (cf. the advertising cycle, c). For a similar, independently arrived-at viewpoint, see Blattberg and Jeuland (1980). This is why, in discussing MaxEF/c in Chapter 3's Section 3.2.2 previously, it was pointed out that exposures beyond MEF may not necessarily be wasted except in "immediate" reach patterns.

Applying the carryover "constant" of $.9^w$, where w is the number of weeks since the end of the cycle, c, a table can be constructed showing the adjusted levels of MEF/c necessary to maintain active effective reach (AER) at the level of the effective reach (ER/c) attained during the ad cycle, for hiatus periods of 1 up to 5 weeks. The calculation of the adjusted MEF/c is made by dividing the original MEF/c by $.9^w$ and then rounding up to the next whole number. These estimates are given in Table 4.1. The carryover-adjusted MEF/c values can easily be calculated for other values of the carryover constant and hiatuses longer than 5 weeks.

Looking ahead to Chapter 7, which introduces media scheduling software called Media Mania, it should be noted that the desired adjusted MEF/c can be read off Media

Mania's exposure distribution (ED), which gives the proportions of those reached at each frequency level *during* the cycle. For example, suppose, the original MEF/c estimate is 4/c in a 3-week advertising cycle. Hiatuses of 4 weeks are planned between cycles. To maintain AER at the ER/c number would mean a carryover-adjusted MEF/c value of 7/c, according to Table 4.1, rather than the original 4/c. The media planner would then attempt to maximize reach at 7+/c during each ad cycle, assuming that there is a regular pattern of cycles and hiatuses and a constant MEF requirement.

The reach patterns for which this carryover-adjusted MEF/c computation is necessary are the "flighted" reach patterns: wedge, reverse-wedge/PI, regular purchase cycle (when not every purchase cycle is an advertising cycle), awareness, and seasonal priming. These were discussed in Chapter 2.

4.2. Changes to MEF/c During the Campaign

Contrary especially to "magic number" theories, MEF/c is rarely a constant number during the entire campaign. Most notably, for a new product, if the campaign is working, the MEF/c requirement should steadily reduce. This is the first situation discussed below. Also discussed are so-called "maintenance" campaigns; the use of brand advertising to attract or maintain retailer support; and short-term tactical adjustments to MEF/c.

TABLE 4.1. Adjusted MEF/c levels to maintain active effective reach (AER) at the effective reach (ER) level for various carryover durations

ORIGINAL MEF/c	CARRYOVER-ADJUSTED MEF/c FOR DURATION OF:				
	1 wk	2 wks	3 wks	4 wks	5 wks
1	2	2	2	2	2
2	3	3	3	4	4
3	4	4	5	5	6
4	5	5	6	7	7
5	6	7	7	8	9
6	7	8	9	10	11
7	8	9	10	11	12
8	9	10	11	13	14
9	10	12	13	14	16
10	12	13	14	16	17
11	13	14	16	17	19
12	14	15	17	19	21
13	15	17	18	20	23

4.2.1. MEF/c AND "OUTER" TARGET AUDIENCE CHANGE

Favorable brand switchers (FBSs) and *brand loyals* (BLs) comprise the fringe and the core, respectively, of the brand's sales, and would, if targeted, not be expected to change their status over the course of the campaign. Favorable brand switchers—for regularly purchased products—are not expected to become brand loyals (but rather just to switch-in a little more often) because their purchasing patterns are *routinized* (Howard 1977). Brand loyals are expected to stay loyal and to use the brand a little more often, but again not to change.

However, what if the target audience is an "outer" group—those not buying the brand at present? These outer target audiences, with one exception, are expected to *change* as the campaign works on them—and to change to groups requiring *less frequency*. The target audience requiring the highest MEF/c, new category users (NCUs), in most campaigns is expected to become brand loyals, with a dramatic reduction in MEF from LC + 1 per advertising cycle to 0 (on the target audience correction factor). Similarly, other-brand loyals (OBLs) in most campaigns are expected to convert to loyalty to our brand, with a consequent reduction (on the target audience factor) of 2 exposures per advertising cycle. And although they were not differentiated from other-brand loyals in the target audience correction factor, other-brand switchers (OBSs) could be reduced by about 1 exposure per advertising cycle should they become routinized favorable brand switchers and definitely if they become brand loyals.

The one exception to reducing MEF/c for outer target audiences is the *shifting reach* pattern. This *always* targets NCUs and thus MEF/c has to stay constant.

The media planner's task regarding *individual* continuity over multiple advertising cycles in the advertising period is to estimate when the shift to lower required MEF should be made. The reliable way to do this is by continuously tracking the campaign (Sutherland 1993). If the campaign is not tracked, then judgment has to be employed (as in the wedge reach pattern, in which frequency is progressively reduced with each advertising cycle).

4.2.2. "MAINTENANCE" AND "INNER" TARGET AUDIENCES

A common error in media plans for established brands is to revert to "maintenance weight" during the media plan (a low *rate* of GRPs, such as about 30 GRPs a week). The low weight is employed during what would otherwise, in a *flighted* pattern, be *hiatus* periods of no advertising. This produces a *GRP or spending* pattern called "pulsing"; see, for instance, Simon's (1982) ADPULS media model. However, the *reach* pattern of so-called maintenance weight could be anything. Expenditure patterns do not correspond with reach patterns, which is why they were shown separately in the figures in Chapter 2. Maintenance weight is very likely to depart from the planned reach pattern.

"Maintenance weight" is justifiable only if it contributes to retailer support advertising (see below) or if the GRPs are delivered with enough frequency (actually a high enough *rate*, MEF/c) to at least provide MEF to the "inner" target audiences of favorable brand switchers and brand loyals. If this maintenance MEF effect can't be demonstrated, then you're better off stopping advertising altogether from flight to flight (that is, using *true* flighting as opposed to pulsing) and spending the money in the flights themselves where it will increase *effective* reach.

4.2.3. RETAILER SUPPORT

You might, as a manufacturer, be able to advertise below MEF in a particular advertising cycle when the *retailer also is advertising the brand*. In this case, the manufacturer's extra advertising, even at low frequency, may help to achieve total MEF. Some continued advertising, even in a weak market area, can help to convince retailers that the brand is being supported in the area and thus is still deserving of shelf space and perhaps special display. Because of the undeniable importance of display to the sales of products sold through retailers, this continued advertising can be vital.

However, "retailer conviction" advertising differs from the previous situation of "MEF top-up" advertising. Because retailer conviction advertising will be below MEF for consumers, it is advisable to place it in media or media vehicles to which *the retailer will be exposed* while occupying his or her out-of-store role as a private consumer. Retail attention to the brand could then maintain sales even though the advertising is not, except by its influence on retailers.

4.2.4. SHORT-TERM TACTICAL ADJUSTMENTS IN FREQUENCY

"Short-term" here is used to mean less than a year. "Tactical" means within the reach pattern and MEF/c levels that constitute the media strategy. The overall reach pattern for the year should be adjusted to accommodate *known* events throughout the budgeting year. (Seasonality is excluded here, as it has already been discussed as a reach pattern in terms of balancing low competitive interference before the seasonal peak or peaks against increased category need during the peak or peaks.) Most often these known events consist of promotion dates to consumers, or special promotions to the trade.

With promotion dates to *consumers*, the important tactic is to shift the *timing* of advertising exposures so that they precede the promotion dates and create a "ratchet effect" (Moran 1978) by priming the prospective buyer's brand attitude going into the promotion. This should cause the brand's *value equity* (Moran 1976) to temporarily increase and the promotion to thereby produce more sales. Note that the MEF/c requirement remains the same, so more frequency is not needed, but rather frequency that *precedes* the promotion date.

With special promotions to the *trade*, as mentioned previously, advertising to consumers is used in many cases to impress distributors that the brand is being given strong consumer support at the same time as the trade drive. Some concentration of exposures within the *consumer* advertising cycle leading up to the *trade* promotion can add to this impression. As far as possible, use media vehicles that the retailer also is exposed to.

4.2.5. VERY SHORT-TERM SCHEDULING

The wise advertiser, in addition to making short-term adjustments for known events, will want to keep some reserve frequency, and thus part of the budget, for very short-term actions and reactions.

The most important of these very short-term contingencies is *response to a leading competitor*. Unanticipated competitive actions, such as the surprise launch date of a new campaign or even a new brand, have the effect of raising our brand's MEF/c under three circumstances: (1) when the target audience is new category users (for example, for personal computers); (2) when brand recall is the brand awareness objective (for example, for airlines or for computers, especially with "outer" target audiences); or (3) when the brand attitude strategy is transformational (for example, new cars, soft drinks). All these use the LC + 1 adjustment, so if the "LC" increases advertising, you should too.

If the target audience is not new category users, and the communication objectives are brand recognition with an informational brand attitude strategy, the "LC" term doesn't enter the calculation and *no reaction* would be the appropriate reaction. Many supermarket and drug store (fmcg) products are in this classification and should *not* worry about competitive levels of advertising or their "share of voice" (see Rossiter and Percy 1997, chapter 20, for more on this).

Another very short-term circumstance is caused by *variation in supply*. Just as a factory breakdown or distributor problem could cause advertising to be withdrawn that otherwise would be wasted, a factory over-run or large purchase of stock could require extra advertising to stimulate demand. For the brand that already is advertising at MEF/c, this extra advertising would be used to increase the number reached at MEF, or perhaps to attract an outer, higher-MEF target audience.

An opposite very short-term variable that affects a surprising number of products and services is *variation in demand* caused by the *weather*—not seasonal patterns but rather unexpected daily or weekly weather variations. Unseasonable rain can cause the demand for umbrellas and raincoats to skyrocket. Unseasonable fine weather can boost sales of house-and-garden products. Among the products most affected by daily variations in weather are foods and beverages such as soup, salads, soft drinks and ice cream. The increase in category need doesn't change the frequency required to direct choice toward a particular brand. Rather, it temporarily shortens the purchase cycle, thus pushing the frequency *rate* up. Because there is usually a corresponding decrease during opposite weather patterns, the overall effect is to keep total advertising frequency constant while simply varying its timing.

A last very short-term variable is to try to achieve "recency," that is, to achieve exposures as close as possible to (just prior to) the individual's purchase decision. It has long been known, and as the discussion of advertising carryover earlier made clear, that both frequency and recency are important determinants of advertising effects. However, the quest for recency (advocated, for instance, by Ephron 1995 and Jones 1995) is much oversimplified, and it certainly should not replace the implementation of the appropriate reach pattern and the focus on MEF/c. Some reach patterns, notably those for new product launches—blitz, wedge, reverse-wedge/PI, and short-term fad—simply will not work unless the MEF/c is attained and there is no way that a single recent OTS can substitute for frequency (see Roberts 1996 or Cowling 1997 for evidence of new and relaunched fmcg brands' response to frequency). For the regular purchase cycle reach pattern, where recency would seem to be highly relevant, the spread of modern shopping patterns makes it almost impossible to guarantee an exposure the day before purchase without also running the ad at virtually daily frequency to everyone, which would not be affordable (and see Reichel and Wood 1997 for evidence that the slight day-before-purchase advantage weakens very sharply if the exposure happens to arrive two days before: +23 percent brand share gain if 1 day before, +16 percent if 2 days, +13 percent if 7 days, and a flat 10 percent if up to 21 days before purchase). The awareness reach pattern has *no* predictable purchase time, so recency can't be applied when this pattern is used. The shifting reach pattern automatically uses recency (but with concentrated MEF/c *frequency*) to those prospects who happen to have the category need, that is, who are "in the market" at that time. Finally, the seasonal priming reach pattern doesn't need to use recency, as a short-term blitz is used at the start of the seasonal peak or peaks. Overall, then, the ideal of "recency" is either automatically accounted for in the reach pattern, or else is impractical and should not direct focus away from MEF/c.

This chapter has provided a detailed explanation of how to decide the effective frequency level or levels to be placed in the selected reach pattern. But how is the reach pattern and the required frequency—the media strategy—achieved? This is media plan implementation, the subject of the remainder of the book.

CHAPTER 5

MEDIA SELECTION

Having decided on the media strategy, it now has to be implemented as a media plan. The three stages of media plan implementation are media selection, media vehicle selection, and construction of the schedule of advertising insertions in the vehicles. This chapter covers media selection (media type selection). Chapter 6 examines media vehicle selection, from media data to strategic rules, and Chapter 7 provides media models to choose the optimal schedule.

Media selection—in terms of broad *types* of media, such as TV, radio, newspapers, and so forth—is usually decided early in the advertising campaign planning process, and it is decided by the advertiser and the agency's account team, rather than by the media planner alone.

This is because the selection of a media type or several media types (such as a primary medium and one or more secondary or support media) is thought to depend on the advertiser's budget and the creative requirements of the campaign to be employed. However, neither of these decisions is as straightforward as it may seem. The alternative media types are actually a lot closer in terms of cost than is generally realized. To equal the household reach of national TV with another medium, for instance, would require advertising placements in numerous radio stations, or the purchase of advertising space in newspapers in all of the major cities. Furthermore, as explained in Chapter 3's MEF/c formula, with typically "low attention" media such as radio, approximately double the number of advertising insertions have to be bought to achieve similar advertising attention levels to those achieved in "high attention" media such as TV and newspapers. Cost, therefore, should not be the main basis of media type selection.

The second commonly-used basis for media selection, the medium's "fit" with creative, is certainly important but the notion of fit is oversimplified. This chapter identifies exactly what "fit" means—first in terms of pre-classification of media types and then more specifically for mass media selection.

5.1. Pre-classification of Media Types

Much is heard nowadays of the "explosion" in media options. However, this mainly refers to the large increase in the number of *vehicles* within media types. TV, radio and print media are all "fragmenting," with more vehicles now available, and increasingly so, to suit people's individual leisure patterns and shopping needs. At the broader level of media *types*, however, the options are pretty much standard, although there has been the recent addition of the Internet (World Wide Web) as an advertising medium.

Media types can be pre-classified according to campaign purpose. Basically, there are three broad types of media, by campaign purpose:

1. *Mass media* – these are used to create or build brand awareness and brand attitude so as to generate brand purchases over a long period (where the brand may be a company or a particular product or service marketed by the company).
2. *Point-of-decision (P-O-D) media* – these are much narrower media which reach the prospect at the point-of-purchase or point-of-use, to stimulate immediate brand purchase, or brand usage (promotions are mainly placed in these media).
3. *Direct-response (DR) media* – these are media which carry direct-response marketing offers that attempt to sell the product or service outright. Direct-response ads can be placed in *mass* media; or in *dedicated* and almost exclusively direct-response media, which are: direct mail, directories, telephone (telemarketing), and TV or PC interactive (web advertising).

5.1.1. MASS MEDIA

When the campaign's purpose is to create or build brand awareness and brand attitude to aid long-term brand purchases, it is almost impossible to look past mass media. P-O-D media are too narrow and are exposed too late in the decision process to build brand awareness and attitude. Direct-response media, on the other hand, are not aimed so much at building brand awareness and brand attitude for the long term (this would be a very expensive way of doing so). Rather, they attempt to create awareness immediately (or capitalize on previous company awareness), generate a convincing attitude toward the product or service immediately, and thereby to sell the product or service outright. DR media, quite evidently, are largely an alternative to personal selling.

Mass media will always be the choice for mass-marketed products and services, and they are also the fastest means for other products and services to create or increase awareness and attitude when personal selling or DR media will be used to finalize the sale.

There are seven mass media options: television, cable television, radio, newspapers, magazines, stationary outdoor and posters, and mobile outdoor and posters. It is worthwhile to distinguish regular television and cable television (or, in some countries, satellite television), because of the availability of infomercials on the latter. Another functional distinction (Rossiter and Percy 1987, 1997) is between "stationary" outdoor and poster media (where the prospect and ad are stationary relative to one another, allowing a longer advertising message) and "mobile" outdoor and poster media (where either the prospect is passing the ad, as with highway billboards, or the ad is passing the prospect, as with bus exterior posters, and for which only short advertising messages are possible). Also, it is worth noting that some products are launched via publicity rather than advertising, a well-known example being (Paul) Newman's Own salad dressing. If so, the publicity takes on the characteristics of the main medium in which the publicity is placed, such as television or magazines.

In Section 5.2, it will be seen that particular communication capacities are the factors used to select one or more mass media for the campaign. In Section 5.3, media selection for small-audience advertisers will be considered which will include local or specialized rather than "mass" media although physically the media are the same.

5.1.2. POINT-OF-DECISION (P-O-D) MEDIA

P-O-D media are now so numerous and specialized that they are a big cause of the perceived media explosion. Exterior store signage and window displays, interior store displays and on-shelf promotions, and free-standing inserts (FSIs) in newspapers are some of the many point-of-*purchase* media; and packaging, home or office product containers or service stickers, and recipe or do-it-yourself books are some of the inventive point-of-*use* media. Point-of-purchase and point-of-use are the two main subtypes of P-O-D media.

There is only one appropriate way to select P-O-D media (if the campaign's purpose is to stimulate immediate purchase or usage intentions) and that is by target audience reach at the time and location of the decision. A behavioral sequence model of the product or service category decision process (Rossiter and Percy 1997) can be constructed to identify the best P-O-D media opportunities.

5.1.3. DIRECT-RESPONSE (DR) MEDIA

Another cause of the perceived media explosion is, of course, the increase in direct marketing—specifically, 1-step direct response advertising in various media. (Excluded here are so-called 2-step or "double duty" ads in which a phone number or website address is *added* to a brand awareness-and-attitude ad, to capture inquiries. An inquiry is the first of two steps to a possible sale, the second being purchase. These are *mass media* ads.)

Direct-response (DR) media, in approximate magnitude of advertiser expenditure in the U.S.A., are: telemarketing, direct mail, directories, DR cable television, DR television, DR newspapers, DR magazine, DR radio, and websites (with this new DR medium moving up the list rapidly) to which access is by interactive TV or PC.

Media selection from the DR media alternatives depends largely on the product or service type. Table 5.1 shows how the DR media decision is usually made.

TABLE 5.1. Media selection for direct-response advertising

Product and target audience	Recommended DR media
Any product or service	Direct mail
Product or service category that is well known and doesn't have to be seen	Directories Telephone (telemarketing)
Product or service with broad target audience (no mailing list available)	Newspaper Television (demonstration products)
Product or service whose target audience is well defined by an occupational or other demographic or psychographic readership or listenership group	Magazine Radio Interactive TV or PC (upper income or education)

The criteria for selecting P-O-D and DR media are quite straightforward. This is not the case for mass media. The selection criteria for mass media are examined next.

5.2. Mass Media Selection

Mass media are the natural choice for campaigns whose purpose is to build and reinforce brand awareness and brand attitude. With seven mass media to choose from—television (TV), cable TV, radio, newspapers, magazines, stationary outdoor and posters, and mobile outdoor and posters—mass media selection is best accomplished in two steps.

The first step is to apply a communication capacity or "creative fit" screening procedure to reduce the number of mass media options, eliminating those that clearly don't allow fit and seriously questioning any that would have creative limitations. This screening procedure is the subject of Sections 5.2.1 to 5.2.3. Quite often, however, several options will remain, necessitating a second step if one primary medium is to be selected.

The second step, assuming two or more primary mass media options remain, each allowing creative fit, is to select the medium that offers the largest target audience reach in relation to cost. This is discussed in Section 5.2.4 in conjunction with primary and secondary media selection.

There are three "creative fit" factors to consider in mass media selection: visual capacity (needed for brand recognition), frequency capacity (needed for brand recall and also for low risk/transformational advertising), and message processing capacity (needed for high risk/informational advertising). The three factors are discussed next along with suitable mass media options.

5.2.1. VISUAL CAPACITY

Campaigns which have as a communication objective the establishment or maintenance of *brand recognition* must normally use media that offer visual capacity. *Visual* brand recognition—of the brand's package or the company's logo—is the main brand awareness objective for many consumer products (especially supermarket and drug store products) and also for retail establishments (for walk-by or drive-by customers). Visual brand recognition is also the brand awareness objective for direct-response advertising (notably direct mail or web advertising) where the consumer or customer is making an immediate purchase decision. Here, however, the focus is on visual brand recognition achieved via mass media.

Visual capacity eliminates radio from consideration and makes color a requirement if newspapers are being considered. For creating or building brand recognition, the principal media types are shown in Table 5.2. They are television, cable television, *color* newspapers, magazine, stationary outdoor and posters, and mobile outdoor and posters. The two types of outdoor and posters offer sufficient reach of about 85 percent of adults over a 30-day period with just enough frequency to be included for brand recognition.

TABLE 5.2. Brand recognition
(visual) media options

Television

Cable television

Newspapers (if color)

Magazines

Stationary outdoor and posters

Mobile outdoor and posters

The exception to the need for visual capacity occurs when *verbal* brand-name recognition is sufficient for customer decision-making, as in recognizing the name of a wine on a restaurant menu, for instance, or recognizing the name of the company when a salesperson calls. Radio *is* suitable for creating or building verbal brand recognition, as are all the other mass media. Usually, however, in these situations, brand *recall* is the main awareness objective, with verbal brand-name recognition assumed to follow if the name is recallable. Brand recall requires frequency capacity, as explained next.

5.2.2. FREQUENCY CAPACITY

Campaigns that have *brand recall* as a brand awareness communication objective require *frequency capacity*. Frequency capacity is crucial when creating or building brand recall and is also desirable for brand recall maintenance, especially in highly competitive product categories when the brand may need to use dominance (see Chapter 1) to counteract competition. Frequency is necessary because brand recall requires that the brand name be very strongly associated with the product category or "category need" in the prospect's mind and this association requires *repetition* (Rossiter and Percy 1997). Thus, the medium or media selected for brand recall purposes must be capable of delivering a reasonably high (rate of) frequency to the target audience.

The high-frequency media for brand recall are television, cable television, radio, newspapers, and, depending on the target audience, stationary and mobile outdoor and posters. Brand recall media are listed in Table 5.3. These media can deliver almost daily frequency of the advertising. People may not watch television, listen to the radio, or read newspapers every day but they can usually be reached by these media at least several times a week. Outdoor and posters become a media option *only* if the target audience has a high proportion of commuters who will regularly pass these sites.

Of the mass media, magazines cannot deliver frequency quickly enough to be considered when brand recall is the communication objective.

TABLE 5.3. Brand recall
(high-frequency) media options

Television

Cable television

Radio

Newspapers

Stationary outdoor and posters (commuters)

Mobile outdoor and posters (commuters)

5.2.3. MESSAGE PROCESSING CAPACITY

The previous two factors, visual capacity and frequency capacity, are the main determinants of media selection for the two forms of brand awareness: brand recognition and brand recall, respectively. In addition to brand awareness, all campaigns have a *brand attitude* objective. The brand attitude objective is to create, increase, maintain, modify, or change the target audience's evaluation of the brand (see Rossiter and Percy 1997 for detailed coverage of these objectives). However, it is actually the brand attitude *strategy*, rather than the brand attitude objective, that has to be considered in media selection. Brand attitude strategy requires, in the medium or media selected, sufficient *message processing capacity*.

Brand attitude strategy depends on whether the brand purchase decision, for the target audience, is low risk or high risk (often called low or high "involvement" because high-risk decisions demand more involvement in processing the advertising message) and whether the major motivation for choosing the brand is informational (sometimes called "rational" but actually referring to one of the negatively-originated "relief" motives, namely problem removal, problem avoidance, incomplete satisfaction, mixed approach-avoidance, or normal depletion) or transformational (sometimes called "emotional" but actually referring to positively-originated, positive emotional appeals to one of the "enhancement" motives, namely sensory gratification, intellectual stimulation or mastery, or social approval). The combination of low versus high purchase risk and informational versus transformational purchase motivation forms the four brand attitude quadrants in the Rossiter-Percy grid (those seeking more detail on this grid are referred to Rossiter, Percy and Donovan 1991, and Rossiter and Percy 1997). Managers are cautioned against the use of the well-known FCB grid, which is superficially similar but classifies whole product categories instead of brands and does not take into account the brand purchase risk for the target audience. Brand purchase risk will be low for target audiences that will be making repeat purchases of the target brand, namely the brand's loyal buyers or favorable switchers, but is likely to be high for all other target audiences, namely loyal buyers of another brand who will have to be induced to try or re-try the target brand, or those purchasing in the category for the first time. The four brand attitude strategy alternatives are therefore: low risk/informational, low risk/ transformational, high risk/informational, or high risk/transformational. The relevant brand attitude strategy for the campaign is decided before preparing the creative (the ads or promotions) for the campaign, so the medium or media can then be selected to accommodate the strategy in terms of message processing capacity.

The media options for these four brand attitude strategies depend on the respective strategies' message processing requirements. Advertising for *low risk/informational* brand choices typically only has to convey one or two benefit claims and this can be accomplished in *any* mass medium. These are listed in Table 5.4.

TABLE 5.4. Low risk/informational
brand attitude strategy media options

Television

Cable television

Radio

Newspapers

Magazines

Stationary outdoor and posters

Mobile outdoors and posters

Advertising for *low risk/transformational* brand choices has more limited media options. Specifically, if the transformational brand "image" requires visual advertising, then radio is eliminated from consideration and, for newspapers, color is usually required. But transformational campaigns, especially for new brands or brands that are trying to build their image, usually require *high frequency*, and this invokes the frequency capacity limitation (discussed earlier for brand recall) and eliminates magazines. It also limits outdoor and posters to commuter audiences. Table 5.5 lists the appropriate media for the low risk/transformational brand attitude strategy.

TABLE 5.5. Low risk/transformational
brand attitude strategy media options

Television

Cable television

Radio (unless visual required)

Newspapers (color usually required)

Stationary outdoor and posters (commuters)

Mobile outdoor and posters (commuters)

Advertising for *high risk/informational* brand choices is the most restrictive in terms of media selection because, nearly always, a detailed message has to be processed by the prospective buyer. Industrial advertising and consumer durables advertising are two forms of advertising for which high risk (high involvement) messages are almost always employed. The media options for high risk/informational product advertising must allow sufficient processing time by the prospective buyer. The high cost of long commercials eliminates television and radio as *mass* media advertising for these types of products (although they can of course be used for direct-response ads in off-peak time slots). The options are listed in Table 5.6.

TABLE 5.6. High risk/informational
brand attitude strategy media options

Cable television
Newspapers
Magazines
Stationary outdoor and posters (commuters)

Advertising for *high risk/transformational* brand choices may be allocated across *two* media: one that can build brand awareness quickly and can achieve the transformational purpose (typically television) and the other that can achieve the "informational underlay" that often accompanies the high risk aspect of the brand choice (typically magazines or newspapers). The informational underlay requires more extensive processing time. Advertising for new cars, for instance, uses this combination of two media to deliver transformation then information. There are, however, other options for the transformational-only purpose and the informational underlay purpose (when needed). These are summarized in Table 5.7.

TABLE 5.7. High risk/transformational brand attitude strategy media options

Transformational only	Plus informational underlay
Television	Television (will need secondary informational medium)
Cable television	Cable television (long commercials or infomercials)
Radio (unless visual required)	Radio (long commercials)
Newspapers (color usually required)	Newspapers
Magazines	Magazines
Stationary outdoor and posters (commuters)	Stationary outdoor and posters (commuters)
Mobile outdoor and posters (commuters)	

5.2.4. THE CAMPAIGN'S PRIMARY AND SECONDARY MEDIA

The primary medium for the campaign must be one that can accomplish *both* the brand awareness objective and the brand attitude strategy. Many campaigns use only one medium, the primary medium, whereas other campaigns use a primary medium and one or several secondary or support media. These secondary or support media are added to the campaign because of their particular ability to *additionally* deliver *one* of these factors—either the brand awareness objective *or* the brand attitude strategy.

Secondary media are used by larger advertisers when one of the brand's communication effects (brand awareness or brand attitude) can be efficiently "boosted" by the addition of a secondary medium. The selection of a secondary medium, or sometimes the selection of two or more secondary media, can be made from the specific-effect tables (Tables 5.2 to 5.7 earlier) to increase brand recognition or brand recall, or to assist in achieving the relevant brand attitude strategy.

Primary media options for mass-media advertisers are identified from the foregoing tables by listing the media that can deliver the specific type of brand awareness and the specific type of brand attitude strategy. A summary table of primary media options is shown in Table 5.8. It can be seen that the options become reduced when these communication "fit" criteria are jointly applied, and further reduced if the limitations (parenthesized) apply.

TABLE 5.8. Primary media options for the mass-media advertiser

BRAND RECOGNITION AND:			
LOW RISK/INFO	LOW RISK/TRANS	HIGH RISK/INFO	HIGH RISK/TRANS
Television	Television	Cable television	Television (will need secondary medium if information underlay)
Cable television	Cable television	Newspaper (color)	Cable television
Newspapers (color)	Newspapers (color)	Magazines	Newspapers (color)
Magazines	Stationary outdoor and posters (commuters)	Stationary outdoor and posters (commuters)	Magazines
Stationary outdoor and posters	Mobile outdoor and posters (commuters)		Stationary outdoor and posters (commuters)
Mobile outdoor and posters			Mobile outdoor and posters (commuters) (will need secondary medium if informational underlay)

BRAND RECALL AND:

LOW RISK/INFO	LOW RISK/TRANS	HIGH RISK/INFO	HIGH RISK/TRANS
Television	Television	Cable television	Television (will need secondary medium if informational underlay)
Cable television	Cable television	Newspapers	Cable television
Radio	Radio (unless visual required)	Stationary outdoor and posters (commuters)	Radio (unless visual required)
Newspapers	Newspapers (color)		Newspapers (color)
Stationary outdoor and posters (commuters)	Stationary outdoor and posters (commuters)		Stationary outdoor and posters (commuters) (will need secondary medium if informational underlay)
Mobile outdoor and posters (commuters)	Mobile outdoor and posters (commuters)		Mobile outdoor and posters (commuters) (will need secondary medium if informational underlay)

Primary Media Selection by Target Audience Reach and Cost—and Strategy

As mentioned at the outset of Section 5.2 on mass media type selection, and as evident now from Table 5.8, screening for communication capacity or creative fit—while essential—may still leave two to six media eligible for primary medium consideration.

A single primary medium can be selected in a second step based on target audience reach and cost, taking the *media strategy* into account. Marketing managers and media planners all too often use stereotyped beliefs about target audience reach and cost to choose a primary medium or rule out others without careful consideration of the media strategy. Thus, for instance, cable TV may be thought best for reaching up-market households, or radio may be regarded as a less costly alternative to television for a mass-market audience, or outdoor and posters may seem best for reaching teenagers.

This method of selection should be resisted. Media data (see Chapter 6) on target audience reach and typical media vehicle costs should be consulted—together with the intended reach pattern (Chapter 2) and effective frequency requirements per ad cycle (Chapter 3). When arrived at properly, primary medium selection is not a simple decision.

For instance, re-visit the stereotyped examples above but now consider the media strategy. It may turn out that whereas cable TV does provide good up-market household reach, program viewing on cable TV is too scattered should the reach pattern and MEF/c require high frequency; in this case, programs on regular TV or a selection of up-market magazines might be a better choice because both deliver higher frequency. Radio might appear less expensive than TV but its low attention properties (see Chapter 3's MEF/c formula) might mean many more insertions of the advertising would be needed to achieve the desired effective reach, making TV not much more expensive and with fewer separate station buys to negotiate. Outdoor and posters might seem to be a good choice for reaching teenagers but if the campaign calls for reach emphasis rather than frequency emphasis, a quick blitz on TV programs in prime time which draw a large family audience might well produce higher teenage reach without wasted frequency and end up costing less.

A conscientious media planner would take these complex considerations into account in selecting the primary medium (where most of the client's budget will be spent). Nevertheless, it is always good practice to "run the numbers" in support of the recommended media type or types when there are several alternatives. Surprisingly often, the best choice is not obvious initially, or if it was, it's now confirmed.

5.3. Media Selection for Small-audience Advertisers

Small-audience advertisers mainly comprise two categories: business-to-business advertisers (some of them not so small as companies but with a small, specialized target audience) and local retail advertisers (this includes large retailers running local campaigns at branches of their stores). Such advertisers can rarely justify the use of mass media advertising. However, they have other very effective *non*-mass media to choose from that provide local or specialized-audience reach. The media options for these two advertiser categories are examined below.

5.3.1. BUSINESS-TO-BUSINESS ADVERTISERS

Business-to-business advertisers usually advertise in business magazines, trade publications, or by direct mail, depending on the size of their target audience. Media selection for business-to-business advertisers is shown in Table 5.9. It should be noted that the print media shown are capable of delivering brand recognition and (if the business magazines or trade publications are frequent enough) brand recall, as well as high risk/informational brand attitude strategy, the usual strategy for business products and services.

As the table indicates, although there are no hard rules for this, the minimum audience size for advertising in business magazines would be about 1000 prospects. At the other extreme, less than 100 prospects is usually too small an audience to advertise to and instead the advertiser should rely on personal selling, with pamphlets or brochures as sales aids. Business-to-business advertisers can also add direct-response media according to their product or service and audience types (see previous Table 5.1).

TABLE 5.9. Media selection for business-to-business advertisers

Size of target audience (number of prospects)	Recommended media
Larger (> 1000)	Business magazines
	Trade publications
	Direct mail
Moderate (100 – 1000)	Trade publications
	Direct mail
Smaller (<100)	None (use personal selling, with pamphlets or brochures as sales aids)

5.3.2. LOCAL RETAIL ADVERTISERS

Local retail advertisers use advertising to attract customers to the store or retail outlet. A retail chain can use mass media such as television, radio, or newspapers to advertise products or services that are common across locations, but an individual store in that chain wishing to advertise locally or a truly local retailer would have too much wasted reach and incur too high an expense to use mass media. Local media are much more appropriate, as listed in Table 5.10.

TABLE 5.10. Media options for local retail advertisers

Display ad in local telephone directory
Suburban newspapers
Local outdoor or posters
Handbills or fliers
Direct mail (if database marketing is worthwhile)

All these local media can deliver brand recognition, but only suburban newspapers have enough frequency capacity to deliver brand recall unless handbills or fliers are very frequently distributed by the retailer; all these local media can carry quite detailed messages for the high risk/informational brand attitude strategy typically needed to attract retail patronage. Local telephone directories are perhaps an exception for the multi-product retailer but local retailers cannot afford *not* to have a listing, and preferably a display ad, in the local directory.

Direct mail is conditionally listed as a local retail medium in the table. This medium should be used if it seems worthwhile for the local retailer to practice database marketing. For frequently-purchased retail-product stores (grocery stores, newsagents, drug stores), database marketing is neither necessary nor practical. However, for retailers whose products or services are on a longer purchase cycle (such as dental practices, furnishings, clothing stores), database marketing, either via continued direct mail or by telemarketing, is certainly worthwhile.

5.4. Summary of Media Selection

The first decision in media selection depends on whether the campaign is going to be a brand awareness-and-attitude-building campaign (calling for mass media); a brand purchase or usage-stimulation campaign (using point-of-decision, or P-O-D, media), or a direct marketing campaign (using direct-response, or DR, media).

Tables are provided for mass media selection based on creative "fit": specifically, in terms of the brand awareness objective and the brand attitude strategy. Media types differ in their visual capacity (for brand recognition), frequency capacity (for brand recall and low risk/transformational advertising), and message processing capacity (for high risk/informational advertising and for high risk/transformational advertising, with and without an informational underlay). The primary medium must be able to deliver total fit. In the event of several media types being suitable on fit, the final choice is made in terms of target audience reach *and* the medium's ability to accommodate the media strategy. When analyzed strategically with media data (see Chapter 6), the choice of a primary medium will usually be clear. Large advertisers will also add one or two secondary or support media if these can efficiently boost the brand's awareness *or* attitude.

Small-audience advertisers will usually not use mass media as there is too much wasted reach and the cost is too high. Tables of non-mass media are provided for the two main categories of small-audience advertisers: business-to-business advertisers and local retail advertisers.

All advertisers may from time to time, or even exclusively, employ P-O-D or DR media. The main options for these are tabled in the chapter.

CHAPTER 6

MEDIA DATA, DUPLICATIONS, AND STRATEGIC RULES

Translation of the media strategy into an actual media plan or schedule requires a selection of media vehicles—particular TV programs, particular radio stations and times, national, local, or suburban newspapers, and so forth, within the designated media type or types. To select media vehicles, you will need to obtain *media data*, from panels or surveys that are available to media planners by subscription. Some sources of data are better than others, and these differences need to be pointed out. These data will include specific media vehicle ratings (the number and percent of people reached by each vehicle). The media data may also include a very important set of data called *duplications* (the overlap of people reached by the vehicle over occasions and the overlap of people across vehicles). If duplication data aren't available, they can be approximated as shown in this chapter.

Also necessary before going to the computer to implement the schedule (covered in Chapter 7) is that you understand and apply the *strategic rules* of media vehicle selection. As will be shown, these strategic rules or guidelines go a long way toward correctly implementing the media strategy even if you don't use a computer, although a computer model provides valuable precision and optimization to implement the strategy at lowest cost.

6.1. Media Data

Media data will be described first in the terms of the three usual sources, which are separate: television, print, and radio. With data only from the media side of the equation, not linked to purchase data, target audiences can only be identified *demographically*, to correspond with the demographic profile of product users. This leads to usually imprecise reach of the target audience, especially when target audiences are defined on a brand loyalty basis (Rossiter and Percy 1997). Purchase-linked media data are now available to enable more precision. Some of these data sources provide cross-media data as well as purchase data. The ideal is single-source data, though this has proved methodologically difficult and expensive to provide. An alternative that is growing in popularity is pseudo single-source data. Single-source and pseudo single-source data are both described at the end of this section.

6.1.1. TELEVISION

People Meter Panels
In many countries, television ratings are determined by a people meter panel of homes spread across the nation. For example, in the U.S.A. there are 5000 people meter panel

homes, in New Zealand 440 homes, and in China, a new market for people meters, 300 homes (Green 1997). The sampling procedure for people meter panels in countries with a current or former AGB-based ratings supplier is to select homes at random to represent the country with respect to region, level of TV viewing, size of household, number of TVs in the home, age of main household shopper, presence of children, and several other demographic variables, via a stratification system known as control matrices (Kent 1994).

A people meter is an electronic device that sits on top of the TV set and continually records all the TV's activity. To ensure that the people meter records what the *people* in the house are watching and not just what the TV is doing, householders (those over 4 or 5 years old) use a remote control to "log in" when they are watching TV. Every 15 minutes, the people meter prompts those currently logged in to indicate whether they are still watching the program the TV is tuned to. Each nonportable TV in the home has a people meter attached to it. There is also provision for guests to log in if they watch TV in a people meter home and provision to record VCR viewing in the home. Thus, the people meter system is designed to capture all of the television viewing by all the eligible people in the home. In the early morning, the people meter sends its data by telephone link to the ratings supplier. This information is processed immediately, so ratings for the previous day are available to clients the following morning, usually in the form of minute-by-minute ratings.

People meters are relatively sophisticated but they do rely on compliance by viewers. Non-compliance occurs when someone is watching TV but has not logged in or is logged in but not watching. Most countries check for this with "coincidental surveys" (Danaher and Beed 1993) in which panelists are called and asked "When the telephone just rang, were you watching TV?" The panelist's verbal response is compared with what the people meter says they were doing with respect to TV viewing. Danaher and Beed (1993) showed that about 91 percent of panelists are compliant. Interestingly, of the 9 percent who are noncompliant, about half say they are watching when they are not logged in, while the other half say they are *not* watching but they *are* logged in. The net effect on the people meter audience ratings is that the "overs and unders" cancel out and the people meter ratings are very close to the true ratings for each program.

Diary Panels
Another popular method for measuring TV ratings is the diary panel method. Here, booklets listing each channel and quarter-hour for a week (sometimes longer) are left in the home to be filled out every day by each person aged 11 and older living in the home, with TV viewing by children between the ages of 2 and 10 written in by a parent or guardian. At the end of the week, an interviewer returns to collect the diaries for the household.

An apparent problem with diaries is that respondents may leave them untouched until the last day then fill them in from memory. There is also a bias toward reported viewing of TV shows which might be considered socially acceptable. As a result, programs like evening news shows usually have inflated ratings by the diary method because people think they "always watch the news" or "should watch" when, in fact, they often miss one or two nights; confirming this, in Australia and New Zealand when people meters came on the scene, ratings for evening news shows went down (Beed 1992). Another problem with diaries is that people often under-record their viewing to daytime and late-night television and small (often cable) channels. With the rapid profusion of small channels in the past 10 years, this is clearly a problem for the TV diary method.

6.1.2. PRINT

Face-to-face Surveys

Due to the complexity of print survey questions and the frequent use of show-cards, print media surveys are usually accomplished with face-to-face survey interviews of people aged 10 years or older. The survey design is most often a multi-stage cluster sample whereby clusters are randomly selected across the country and a fixed number of people are interviewed within each cluster. The survey asks each respondent which vehicles he or she has recently read or looked at from a long list of magazines and newspapers.

Two question formats commonly used for weekly *magazines* are:

Q1) "Have you personally read or looked into any issue of (magazine name) in the last seven days—it doesn't matter where?" (Answer: Yes/No)

Q2) "How many different issues of (magazine name) do you personally read or look into in an average month—it doesn't matter where?" (Answer: 0, 1, 2, 3, 4 issues)

Q1 (reach) and Q2 (frequency) employ the "reading habit" method. Danaher (1988) shows how Q1 and Q2 are modified for two-weekly, monthly and two-monthly magazines. Q1 asks for recent reading of "any" issue of the magazine. The accuracy of the response to Q2 is dependent on the respondent's memory. Those who never or always read the magazine should have little difficulty recalling such behavior. Those who occasionally read the magazine are not requested to say in which weeks they read the magazine but just "on average," which should alleviate recall difficulties. Another similar method used in the U.S.A., notably by SMRB (Simmons) and MRI (Mediamark), is the "recent reading" method. Most accurate but rarely used nowadays because of the extensive interview time and the need to provide copies of every magazine and newspaper, or at least the front page of each, is the "through the book" method. Chandon (1976) reviews these alternatives.

For daily and suburban *newspapers*, respondents are asked the same Q1 (for reach), and then for Q2 (frequency) they are asked to recall their reading behavior over the last seven days. For instance, if they are interviewed on a Wednesday, they'll be asked if they read a particular newspaper on the previous Wednesday through Tuesday. Days when the newspaper is not published are omitted from the questioning.

Magazine and newspaper surveys usually include an additional question on the respondent's "sourcing" of the issue. If the person is a subscriber or bought the issue personally from a newsstand or other retail outlet, he or she is designated as a *primary* reader. If it was obtained from someone else or, for instance, seen in a waiting room, he or she is designated as a *passalong* reader. Primary readers are more likely to look right through the magazine or newspaper and therefore have higher attention for exposure to ads (see the vehicle attention factor in Chapter 3's MEF/c formula).

Other Survey Methods
Although most print media surveys employ face-to-face interviewing, telephone interviewing is conducted in some countries, notably the Netherlands, where a "first read yesterday" method is employed, a variant of recent reading. In the U.S.A., Audits & Surveys employs a mail panel for print media measurement, in the expectation that this will yield a better sample of affluent readers who may not agree to a face-to-face interview.

Recalled Reach and Frequency
Print media audience measurement worldwide is therefore mostly based on recall of vehicles read (reach) and recalled reading occasions (frequency). For cost reasons, the recall method dominates, even though it is likely that this method, in comparison with "through the book" recognition to aid recall, may underestimate the reach of "impulse-purchased" magazines and of secondary or "passalong" readership of magazines and newspapers.

6.1.3. RADIO

Diary Panels or Surveys
Radio listening audiences are typically measured by the diary panel method (similar to that used in some countries for television). Diaries are dropped off in randomly selected homes for later pickup. Respondents tick (check off) the appropriate station box in the diary for every quarter-hour of radio they listen to.

Another popular, but less accurate, method used for radio audience measurement is face-to-face or telephone surveys in which respondents are asked to recall their listening (similar to the recall method in most print media surveys) over the past several days.

Brown (1992) reviews the pros and cons of these alternative methods in an international context. He finds diaries to be less than perfect, although preferable to recall methods. The method chosen is usually the best the respective market can afford given the low proportion of total advertising spend that radio attracts.

6.1.4. SINGLE-SOURCE DATA

Media surveys usually concentrate on just one medium or media type at a time (separate samples are interviewed for each medium). For instance, television people meter panels are used for television audience measurement and readership surveys for print media. However, as explained in Chapter 5, advertisers often employ two or more media types in a single campaign, as in integrated communications campaigns. The growing use of *cross-media* campaigns has increased the demand for cross-media audience data. At the same time, advertisers have been seeking a link between media exposure and product and brand usage so as to avoid the need for indirect targeting by demographics.

These trends have given rise to single-source media databases of television, radio and print consumption, together with respondents' product and brand usage. "Single-source" refers to the fact that the same respondents (same sample) provide all the information.

The appeal of single-source data is that media viewers, readers or listeners can be matched *directly* to the products they purchase rather than indirectly matching them through demographics (see Assael and Poltrack 1991, 1993, 1994; Cannon and Seamons 1995; and Cowling 1997). Direct matching usually provides at least 10 percent and usually closer to 30 percent greater accuracy in targeting product buyers (Rossiter and Percy 1997) which results in significant savings in media spend.

Whereas the ideal of single-source data is universally accepted, single-source providers have encountered problems in practice which have led to disaffection by advertisers after much initial interest. Most single-source services, such as Target Group Index in the U.S.A. and Europe, and Morgan Single Source (previously MLI) in Australia, use the diary method to collect the cross-media data and purchase data. For TV, which is the major medium of expenditure for many advertisers, the diary method, as noted, is far less accurate than people meter data. For recording purchase, the diary method also is less accurate than the alternative method of in-store or in-home electronic scanner recording. Cowling (1997) has shown that diary reporting (and, it may be assumed, any survey method that relies on recall) can overstate the market shares of leading brands and number-two brands by almost double and place the reverse error on minor brands and store brands, when validated against household scanner-recorded purchases. Diaries (or surveys) do, however, remain the only method for collecting attitudinal or psychographic data when target audiences are defined by these pre-purchase criteria. Compounding the inaccuracy problem for TV and purchase data has been the belief among advertisers that the enormous amount of diary data required of each respondent may result in poor validity due to respondent fatigue, a belief that most single-source diary providers have not been successful in dispelling.

Combined data-collection methodologies have been tried with the purpose of offering single-source data using the best method for each: people meters for TV viewing, diaries for other media, and electronic scanning of purchases (all from the same households). However, this has proved very expensive and household panel recruitment is also alleged to be a problem. The main U.S. service of this type, Nielsen's HomeScan, was discontinued in 1995. IRI offers its BehaviorScan service for testing advertising and promotion plans in five test market areas in the U.S.A., but these areas are not usually thought to be representative enough for national media plans.

The future for true single-source cross-media and purchase data depends on the ability of suppliers to overcome the above problems, especially regarding data validity and cost. The fact is that, at present, true single-source data are not available, or are not available at a national level, in most countries.

6.1.5. PSEUDO SINGLE-SOURCE DATA

To obtain an approximation to single-source data, without the concerns of excessive respondent burden and high survey costs, recent effort has focused on merging separate media databases to obtain *pseudo* single-source information (Baker, Harris, and O'Brien 1989; Danaher and Rust 1992). The merging procedure is known as "multiple imputation" or, more commonly, as "data fusion."

Pseudo single-source databases are available in the U.K. (by TGI and by Taylor Nelson AGB) and in Australia and New Zealand (by ACNielsen). In the TGI method for this, television viewing data from a people meter panel are fused with a survey that provides data on print media and product use. The merging is achieved by matching respondents on the basis of demographic variables measured in common across both surveys. In the method used by TN AGB and by ACNielsen, people meter panelists "donate" their on-going television viewing data to scanner-recorded-purchase panelists. This fusion is done by asking the purchase panelist for a single-time report of his or her habitual television program viewing and then the computer searches for a donor with the same habits (Roberts 1994a, 1994b). TN AGB is conducting a pseudo single-source validation study with 750 households belonging to *both* panels (pure single-source) and preliminary findings are that the TV fusion method is very accurate (Roberts 1994a; Cowling 1997). Cross-media data on newspaper, magazines, radio and cinema exposure is daily-recorded by the purchase panel.

Not discussed so far are sources of media data for *non-mainstream* media, notably outdoor and posters (the only mass medium that is not routinely surveyed), point-of-decision (P-O-D) media, and dedicated direct-response (DR) media, notably direct mail and Internet websites (see Chapter 5). For these media, pseudo single-source data, via fusion, is the only viable way to include them because they require special, separate surveys.

The advantage of pseudo single-source databases is that survey respondents are questioned only about one media type and the survey method can be customized to the medium (people meters for television, for instance) rather than using an extremely lengthy diary in which respondents have to record all their media exposure and purchases. The disadvantage is that most of these fusion methods assume "conditional independence" among survey respondents. That is, given the matching variables from the respective separate databases, it is assumed that the other measured characteristics (such as TV and print consumption) are independent. Danaher and Rust (1992) showed that such an assumption is often reasonable.

One such set of cross-media information is the duplication between, say, television exposure and radio exposure—for example, the proportion of people exposed to both a particular evening television show and a breakfast radio show. Duplication of audiences is an important concept because it helps shape the basic parameters of the media plan (see Chapter 1): reach, frequency, and continuity. Duplication is discussed in detail in the next section.

6.2. Duplication Within and Between Vehicles

Insertions (of ads) go into a media plan and exposures (to the audience) come out. This is a problem to be solved in media planning because not all insertions are seen or heard by everyone. The complexity in the insertions→exposures problem arises because of *duplication of exposures*. Duplication of exposures is absolutely necessary if the plan is to produce a frequency of exposure greater than 1. There are two types of duplication:

(1)   *Within-vehicle* duplication: For example, how many target audience individuals who saw *60 Minutes* on one particular Sunday also saw it the following week? And the week after? And how many saw one of these *60 Minutes* programs but not the other two? And two but not the other one? The extent of audience duplication within the vehicle, over successive presentations, has to be known in order to calculate how many exposures various individuals might receive.

(2)   *Between-vehicle* duplication: For example, how many target audience individuals who saw *60 Minutes* on a particular Sunday *also* watched the *movie* on CBS that followed? Or watched *Seinfeld* on NBC the following Thursday? Or read *The Wall Street Journal* (cross-media between-vehicle duplication) the following Monday? If your ad is placed in each of these vehicles, the extent of duplication *between* the vehicles has to be known in order to calculate how many exposures various individuals might receive.

Understanding within- and between-vehicle duplications helps gain some insight into the broad planning of a media campaign. For instance, if the media strategy is simply to expose as many people as possible at least once (high reach), then the media vehicles selected should have very little overlap in audience (low between-vehicle duplication). In addition, to minimize *within*-vehicle duplication, each vehicle should have only 1 insertion of the ad. A perfect set of media vehicles for a high reach strategy would have no overlap in audience, in which case the combined reach is simply the sum of the individual ratings for each vehicle. However, across a collection of vehicles it is virtually impossible to have *no* between-vehicle duplication. The key is to measure and manage the between-vehicle duplication rather than ignore it or hope it isn't there.

6.2.1. TYPICAL VEHICLE DUPLICATIONS

The typical magnitudes of within-vehicle and between-vehicle duplications are shown in Table 6.1 for the main media types. In the first column are typical reach percentages (percent of adults aged 18 or older unless indicated more specifically) for that medium's vehicles. In the remaining three columns are *repeat-exposure proportions*, for the different media and, for TV, for various time periods between programs. (Repeat-exposure is one way of showing duplication. It does, though, express a *conditional* probability: the probability of the next event given that the first has occurred. Computerized media programs usually work with *joint* probabilities, as explained shortly.) Note that these are same-medium duplications. Cross-media duplications are discussed later.

One type of duplication, as noted earlier, is *within-vehicle*. In the table, the TV within-vehicle repeat-exposure proportions indicate, for example, that for evening news programs, 54 percent of the people viewing on one night watch the show again the following night. As the time between exposure lengthens from daily to weekly or longer, within-vehicle repeat-exposure levels are smaller. Repeat-exposure levels day-to-day for radio stations are a little lower than one would expect, at 47 percent. The highest day-to-day repeat-exposure is provided by daily newspapers, at 82 percent.

TABLE 6.1. Typical reach and repeat-exposure figures for mass media vehicles (base = all adults 18+ unless otherwise specified)

TELEVISION

	Average rating (% reach)	Proportion repeating: day-to-day			Week to next week	Any 2 weeks in 8-week period
Prime-time program	12.0[a]	.53[b]	Households		.40[c]	.28[d]
			Adults		.41	
			Teens		.27	
			Children		.28	
Evening news program	10.7[a]	.54[b]				
Daytime program	5.0[a]	.61[be]				
Early morning program	4.4[a]	.44[b]				
Late evening program	4.1[a]	.37[b]				
Any two prime-time programs, same channels		.16[e]				
Any two prime-time programs, different channels		.13[e]				
Evening news, different channels		.12[e]				
Daytime, different channel		.05[e]				

RADIO

	Average rating (% reach)	Proportion repeating: day-to-day
Same station	0.7[e]	.47[e]
Different stations		.01[e]

NEWSPAPERS

	Average rating (% reach)	Proportion repeating: day-to-day
Daily paper	46.2[e]	.82[e]
Between papers		~ .00[f]

MAGAZINES

	Average rating (% reach)	Proportion repeating: day-to-day
Same magazine	4.3[e]	.50[e]
Between magazines		.07[e]

OUTDOOR AND POSTER

	Average rating (% reach)	Proportion repeating: day-to-day
Same site	25.0[e]	.50[e]
Between sites		~ .00[f]

INTERACTIVE TV OR PC

	Average rating (% reach)	Proportion repeating: day-to-day
Same site	0.7[g]	.56[g]
Between sites		~ .00[f]

IMPACT SCHEDULES[f] (multiple insertions in same program or issue or site)

TV prime time	.83	Newspaper	.90
TV non-prime	.40	Magazine	.90
Radio	.47	Outdoor and poster	.60

---

[a] ADWEEK'S Marketer's Guide to Media (1994) [b] Headen, Klompmaker and Rust (1979)
[c] Barwise (1986) [d] Ehrenberg and Wakshlag (1987) [e] Stankey (1988) [f] Judgment
[g] Williamson (1996) assuming Internet access for 20 percent of households

Another type of duplication, which was also noted earlier, is *between-vehicle*. Generally, between-vehicle duplications are smaller than within-vehicle duplications. In the table, evening news programs illustrate this for the TV medium, where duplication between different news programs on different channels is 12 percent (between-vehicle), compared with 54 percent within the same news program from night to night (within-vehicle). With TV viewing, there is some degree of program-type loyalty and a slight degree of channel loyalty which push between-vehicle duplications above zero. With other media types, as the table indicates, between-vehicle duplication is typically near zero.

Looking ahead, these figures suggest how a reach strategy (low duplication) or a frequency strategy (high duplication) can be implemented in the media plan.

6.2.2. EXACT VEHICLE DUPLICATIONS

The typical duplications shown in Table 6.1 are useful at the outset of media planning as an aid for vehicle selection. However, precise media plan implementation requires exact vehicle duplication data. Many vehicle-duplication databases are routinely available to ad agencies and media specialist companies (through subscription). These databases are compiled from the media surveys described in Section 6.1 and are increasingly single-source or pseudo single-source, providing cross-media duplications in addition to within-medium duplications.

6.2.3. APPROXIMATE VEHICLE DUPLICATIONS

There may be occasions when you have no access to exact duplication information. This typically arises when you have a media survey which gives ratings for individual vehicles but no duplication data. This is often the case for television and radio surveys, although print media surveys usually report such duplications. In situations where exact duplications are not available, an approximation can be obtained via the Duplication of Viewing Law (Goodhardt and Ehrenberg 1969). This law asserts that the duplication between two different vehicles is proportional to the product of their respective ratings. For instance, if *FRIENDS* rates a 15 and *Seinfeld* rates a 20, then the duplication is proportional to $0.15 \times 0.20 = 0.03$, that is, 3 percent. A concern now is the constant of proportionality. Goodhardt and Ehrenberg (1969) showed it to be close to 1.0 for television shows on different channels and different days, and 1.4 for the same channel on different days. Hence, for instance, the approximate duplication between *FRIENDS* and *Seinfeld* is $1.0 \times 0.03 = 0.03$, that is, 3 percent. (Note that this duplication is the *joint* probability of exposure to both vehicles. It is not the *conditional* probability as reported in Table 6.1.) On the other hand, the approximate duplication *within*-vehicle for two episodes of *Seinfeld* is $1.4 \times 0.2 \times 0.2 = 0.056$, that is, 5.6 percent. Again, this is the joint probability of being exposed to both of two episodes of *Seinfeld*. (The *conditional* probability of viewing a second episode, having seen the first, is $1.4 \times 0.2 \times 0.2 / 0.2 = 0.28$. It may be noted from Table 6.1 previously that this is identical to the "any 2 weeks" figure for adults for prime-time TV programs.) The Duplication of Viewing Law is therefore a useful solution when exact duplications are not available.

6.2.4. CROSS-MEDIA DUPLICATIONS

One set of duplications not presented in Table 6.1 is cross-media (such as TV plus radio plus magazine) duplications. Such information is often not commercially available either, since it requires survey respondents to record their media habits for several media. As noted in Section 6.1.5, media surveys usually concentrate on just one medium at a time, but if true or pseudo single-source data are available then cross-media duplications can be obtained directly.

If you do not have access to true or pseudo single-source data, approximate cross-media duplications can be obtained from the Duplication of Viewing Law in a similar way to that shown for between- and within-vehicle duplications. Although Goodhardt and Ehrenberg (1969) did not give a cross-media duplication constant, the most conservative one to use is 0.94, the lowest of the proportionality constants reported in their paper. This constant is slightly less than 1.0, meaning that the probability that the audience for, say, a TV program will also be listeners to a particular radio station time slot, or read a particular issue of a magazine, is slightly *less* than the "chance" or joint probability obtained from the product of the vehicles' ratings. This is favorable for reach-emphasizing strategies but stands as a caution for "integrated" (cross-media) campaigns if frequency is desired. Integrated campaigns seeking frequency emphasis should have their vehicle overlaps verified by single-source survey data before being approved.

6.3. Strategic Rules

Whereas media planning may have the appearance of being clinical and scientific because of its intense use of data and computers, there is still an art form associated with it. The initial stage of media planning requires considerable judgment, which cannot be dealt with by a computer. The key decision in the selection of media vehicles is the media strategy itself. If the objective is high reach or high frequency or both, what sort of media vehicles should be chosen? To help with this decision, three strategic rules to follow are: the reach rule, the frequency rule, and the reach and frequency rule.

6.3.1. REACH RULE

For high *reach*, buy *many competing* vehicles and place *one or only a small number of ads* in each vehicle. By "competing" vehicles is meant, for example, TV or radio programs in the same time slot but on different channels or stations; or magazines that are close substitutes, such as *Time*, *Newsweek*, and *U.S. News & World Report*. *Competing* vehicles means, of course, that there is less opportunity for between-vehicle duplication and thus frequency will be minimized—and reach maximized—by this factor. This buying strategy will tend to scatter the target audience exposures (the GRPs) very widely. The vehicles can be big or small as long as they have good reach to your target audience.

However, one word of warning about high-rating vehicles is that they tend to also have high repeat-exposure levels, because of an effect known as "double jeopardy" (Goodhardt, Ehrenberg and Collins 1987; Donthu 1995) whereby low-rating vehicles reach a small audience which is also less loyal to the vehicle in terms of repeat-exposures. For prime-time weekly TV programs in the U.S.A., for instance, a program with a 9 rating (9 percent of adults watch it) will have 37 percent of the first-week audience repeat-viewing the next week; a program with a 12 rating (the prime-time average) will have 51 percent; and a program with a 16 rating will have 55 percent (Barwise 1986). Therefore, if you have high-rating vehicles, place only *one insertion* in them to keep the reach high but also to keep the repeat-exposure low.

6.3.2. FREQUENCY RULE

For high *frequency*, buy *multiple insertions* in *few non-competing* vehicles (particularly "strip" vehicles, that is, regularly-repeated vehicles). As long as they have good reach to your target audience, buy *high-rating* vehicles as they tend to have the highest repeat-audiences (this is the double jeopardy effect working *for* you, a "double bonus" in reality). For example, on TV, buy several big serials or quasi-serials such as *E.R.* or *FRIENDS*, which reach 20 to 25 percent of adults with an average episode, although almost any large regular program will do even if it is not a serial; buy evening news on *one channel* if that has good target audience reach. With daily newspapers, buy ad space frequently in the one paper. With weekly or monthly magazines, concentrate only on a few large-audience magazines, such as *Time* or *National Geographic*. This strategy will reduce reach but will maximize frequency (individual continuity of exposures) to the same target audience.

6.3.3. REACH AND FREQUENCY RULE

For high reach *and* high frequency, buy multiple insertions of a moderate number of reasonably big vehicles, especially *strip* vehicles, that are competing. This strategy is a combination of the previous two strategies. The competing vehicles will tend to increase reach, while at the same time multiple insertions in large strip vehicles (repeat-audience) will increase frequency. As will be remembered from the "media balloon" in Chapter 1 (Figure 1.1), reach and frequency have to be traded off for a given budget, and here you are trying to maximize both, within the budget. Generally, maximizing both reach and frequency is an expensive strategy, used most often for new product introductions (via a blitz or wedge reach pattern, see next section).

6.3.4. THE RULES FOR REACH PATTERNS

The various reach patterns described in Chapter 2 require only a few additions to the three general rules because they are, in effect, specific implementations of those rules.

Blitz Pattern. The blitz pattern applies the reach and frequency rule...to the hilt.

Wedge Pattern. The wedge pattern applies the reach and frequency rule initially, then gradually evolves into the reach rule, since frequency is gradually reduced on subsequent flights.

Reverse-wedge/PI Pattern. Try to select a set of vehicles that mainly reach innovators within the target audience initially, and apply the reach rule. On subsequent flights, broaden the vehicles beyond innovators and gradually evolve into the reach and frequency rule.

Fad Pattern. This is a short blitz: use the reach and frequency rule until the peak of the fad's growth, then stop.

Regular Purchase Cycle Pattern. Use the frequency rule, especially if you are going for dominance in particular purchase cycles. If your primary medium is magazines, survey the distribution of target audience reading times, as the lag in reading can greatly displace intended purchase cycle exposures.

Awareness Pattern. This is the reach rule applied to the hilt, with the *same set* of small, or 1-insertion large, competing vehicles bought consistently to produce high individual continuity. Wider-spaced flights with impact scheduling (2 or 3 ads in each program episode or print vehicle issue) are probably more effective than more frequent flights without it because, on each flight, you want to "dose" with MEF everyone reached.

Shifting Reach Pattern. This requires the reach and frequency rule but with the reach part achieved by buying different sets of vehicles each time. Frequency is needed as well because you want to "zap" those with the category need who are reached. Longer or larger ads, or impact scheduling, is therefore recommended.

Seasonal Priming Pattern. Use the reach rule for the prime or primes and then the reach and frequency rule for the seasonal growth phases.

The manager or media planner applying one of these rule-governed reach patterns will find that the number of media vehicle options diminishes quite rapidly—leading to the next step, the placement of insertions. For this, it's best to use a media model, which translates insertions into exposures. Media models are explained in the next chapter, which presents the final stage of media plan implementation.

CHAPTER 7

IMPLEMENTING AND OPTIMIZING THE MEDIA SCHEDULE

The final step of media planning is to implement and optimize the media schedule. The implementation question is: How should *insertions* be scheduled such that these insertions in various vehicles will, in combination, produce the largest effective reach per advertising cycle (reach at MEF or higher, that is, Rk+/c) of *exposures* to the target audience, while keeping within the budget? This is a much more difficult question than it appears—and it is not always well solved in practice. For example, if 20 magazines are available as potential vehicles for your product but you have only enough money to advertise in any six of them, then there are $\binom{20}{6} = 38,760$ possible combinations of these vehicles. Each combination must be examined to see which one will give the maximum effective reach. Obviously, no-one will study 38,760 possible schedules by hand, so computers must be used to help with some of the tedious work of media scheduling.

The purpose of this chapter is to show how to implement and optimize a media schedule—based on the media strategy—by using an appropriate computerized media model.

7.1. Media Models

Media models use media data, consisting of vehicle ratings and either their directly measured or indirectly approximated duplications, to estimate the entire *exposure distribution*, that is, the proportion of people exposed to none, just one, just two, up to all the insertions in the schedule.

Advertising agencies usually use either in-house or syndicated computer software to "plan" their schedules—that is, to examine alternative possible schedules of insertions. A problem with using "black boxes" like this is that users rarely know what sort of assumptions underlie the model(s) implemented by the software. If the model is poor, the resulting reach and frequency estimates will also be poor. Advertising accountability means that today's marketing manager cannot afford inaccurate media models. This is true for the large advertiser spending millions of dollars as well as for the small advertiser for whom every dollar is precious.

The available media models are many and varied and are reviewed by Chandon (1976) and Rust (1986), with some newer models reviewed by Danaher (1992). Most of the available models—including the most popular model, the Beta Binomial model—are not very accurate (Chandon 1976; Danaher 1992; Rice and Leckenby 1986).

To avoid this major problem, this book incorporates a media planning package called Media Mania, designed by the second author. The software package for Media Mania offers two new and highly accurate media models *as well as* the popular but not-very-accurate Beta Binomial model, for comparison. Media Mania is a Windows-based application that is easy to use. In fact, it is designed for marketing managers to use so that they can "see into the black box" and evaluate how their media strategy can best be implemented. It can, of course, also be used by media professionals. The mechanics of installing and using Media Mania are explained in the Appendix. In this chapter, outputs from the software are used to demonstrate the implementation and optimization of schedules to fit various media strategies.

7.2. Media Mania's Models

Media Mania offers three models for performing computations—two very accurate models, Danaher's (1989) Approximate Log-linear model and Danaher's (1991a) Canonical Expansion model, and a standard model for comparison, Metheringham's (1964) Beta Binomial model, which is sometimes referred to as the BBD (for beta-binomial distribution) model. Accuracy is determined for media models by comparing the exposure distribution that they estimate with the actual distribution of exposures. The actual distribution is obtained from a TV-viewing panel or a radio or print survey (see Chapter 6, Section 6.1) by the procedure of "giving" each individual respondent an exposure if they had seen, heard or read the particular vehicle when an insertion would have been placed in it, then physically counting the number of exposures received by each individual across all vehicles and their insertions. This procedure, necessary for validation of media models, is tedious and time-consuming, which is one reason why many media models are *not* validated. The models in Media Mania *have* been validated.

The Approximate Log-linear model is marginally the most accurate overall but is slightly slower computationally for large schedules, that is, when the number of vehicles exceeds six or when there are 4 or more insertions in a vehicle.

The Canonical Expansion model is almost as accurate and is faster, even for large schedules. The Canonical Expansion model is therefore the "default" model in the Media Mania program should a model not be specified by the program user.

The other model included in Media Mania, the Beta Binominal model, is the most popular standard (nonproprietary) model used by media planners. This model is very fast, but is not reliably accurate. It is liable to produce two types of error for all media plans and another type of error for media plans that rely heavily on "strip," or high-loyalty vehicles. The first error is that the Beta Binominal model usually overestimates reach (Leckenby and Rice 1985). Its predicted reach as a percentage of actual reach is often overstated by relatively 10 percent or so—for instance, predicting 55 percent reach when the actual is 50 percent—which deceives the advertiser into thinking the plan is better than it is. Secondly, it can exhibit the logically impossible outcome of reach appearing to be reduced when more insertions are added (Leckenby and Rice 1986). Lastly, because it always produces a "smooth" exposure distribution, it can be very inaccurate for media plans with "strip" vehicles (as recommended in the frequency rule and the reach and frequency rule, see Chapter 6, Section 6.3). With strip (high-loyalty) vehicles, "lumpy" rather than smooth exposure distributions are typical. This is due to, for instance, habitual readership of exactly four issues of a weekly magazine per month (Danaher 1992), or reading all issues of a daily newspaper, or watching the same TV news program every evening. The problem is more acute in print media than in broadcast media, but it occurs in both.

The Beta Binomial model is included mainly so that the manager can see the sort of errors likely to be observed if he or she does not use an accurate model like the Approximate Log-linear model or the Canonical Expansion model.

In Media Mania's software and instructions (Appendix), these models are referred to by slightly abbreviated names, rather than their full technical names. The abbreviated model names are: Approximate Log Linear, Canonical Model, and Beta Binomial.

The Canonical Model, the default option in Media Mania and the faster of the two accurate models, is the model used in the following illustration.

7.3. An Illustration of Reach and Frequency Strategies

This section illustrates the schedule implementation of reach and frequency strategies: it shows the reach rule, the frequency rule, and the reach and frequency rule in operation. The product is a BMW car. For simplicity, the primary and sole medium is television. The budget is $400,000 over a 4-week period, which would amount to a $5.2 million media spend if BMW were to advertise throughout the entire year at a constant monthly rate. The target audience (target group) is men aged 35-plus who live in urban areas and have above-average income (this is a demographic target group, and a reasonable if broad one, although direct matching from single-source or pseudo single-source data, as described in Chapter 6, Sections 6.1.4 and 6.1.5, would enable a more precise identification of luxury car prospects and in particular BMW prospects).

7.3.1. ELIGIBLE VEHICLE SELECTION

The first scheduling task is to identify a list of eligible TV shows. This is best done by examining the first insertion reaches (FIRs) for the target group from a long list of possible programs. Table 7.1 gives FIRs among the target group, in column 3, for 13 television programs. The programs are ranked by their FIR percentages (this will be important for implementing the reach rule). Also shown, in column 4, are these programs' within-vehicle duplications, night-to-night for daily programs and week-to-week for weekly programs (this will be important for implementing the frequency rule). These duplications are conditional probabilities expressed as repeat-exposure percentages, that is, the percent of first-episode viewers who repeat by viewing the second (successive) episode of the program. The first two columns, 1 and 2, show the ratings of the programs among all people 5 years of age and older and the cost of 1 advertising insertion in each program; these data are closely related as costs are mainly determined by total audience ratings. The last column, column 5, shows the cost-per-thousand for the *target group* people (CPMT) for 1 insertion, use of which is discussed below.

TABLE 7.1. Audience and cost information for potential programs
in the media schedules*

Program	Rating (% of all people)	Cost per insertion ($)	FIR (% of target group)	Within-vehicle duplication (%)	CPMT
FRIENDS	19.2	55000	18.2	57	3022.0
Monday Night Football	10.5	41000	15.8	65	2594.9
Seinfeld	12.0	48000	15.0	53	3200.0
60 Minutes	13.7	35000	14.4	48	2430.6
ABC News	12.7	50000	13.5	61	3703.7
NBC Nightly News	11.5	46000	12.7	55	3622.0
20/20	11.3	25500	12.2	44	2090.2
CBS Evening News	10.6	40000	11.6	53	3448.3
Frasier	8.9	43000	10.7	45	4018.7
NYPD Blue	7.5	36000	9.0	42	4000.0
Financial Matters	2.8	15000	4.0	33	3750.0
David Letterman	3.1	18000	3.6	30	5000.0
Larry King	2.0	8000	2.5	25	3200.0

*These are realistic but not actual ratings and costs—they are for illustration only.

CPMT and its Limitations

The most popular vehicle selection statistic used in practice is the (lowest) cost to reach a target viewer/listener/reader, expressed as cost-per-thousand target individuals (CPM Target or CPMT), as in column 5. CPMT is the ratio of cost per insertion to FIR for the target group. A planner who relies strictly on the CPMT selection criterion would tend to advertise just in *60 Minutes, 20/20* and *Monday Night Football*, each of which costs under $3000 per thousand for the target group, or $3.00 per target individual, and would tend to avoid shows like *David Letterman* at $5000 per thousand or $5.00 per target individual. The same number of insertions could cost almost double depending on CPMT of the vehicles.

However, CPMT makes the planner focus too much on cost at the early stage of media planning. Remember that an entire budget is available. It is better to consider costs within the overall budget context and in relation to *estimated profit*. Consider, for instance, a price-promotion TV campaign for BMW which would follow a *reach* strategy. With the discount price, you want to sell a lot of cars to make up total profit. You would therefore select high-reach programs (and aim for high total reach) and ignore CPMT differences.

Consider, alternatively, a high *frequency* strategy, such as for a new BMW model launch. The relevant statistic would then be cost per thousand *effectively reached* (at MEF/c or higher), not simply reached once. CPMT does come into consideration when the frequency requirement is high.

CPERP (Cost Per Effective Reach Point)
Both the reach strategy example and the frequency strategy example, as outlined above, indicate that the target group criterion that the media planner should be trying to *minimize* (keep as low as possible) is *cost per effective reach point*, or CPERP. (Conversely, this could be considered as maximizing the *effective* reach per dollar of budget.) CPERP is the cost per percentage point of effective reach to the target group, in the advertising cycle.

In the reach strategy implementation to follow, CPERP would be cost per percent of R1+/4 weeks, where 4 weeks is the cycle length. In the frequency strategy implementation, CPERP would be cost per percent of R3+/4 weeks. The implementations are based on only one cycle. If several cycles are used in a flighting pattern with carryover, then the criterion for CPERP would be not only cost per effective reach point but also per *active* effective reach point (see Chapter 4) and the cost would be calculated over the cycles and the hiatus periods between them and following the last cycle.

Profit and the audience criterion to be maximized (or cost to be minimized) are further considered in Section 7.4, on optimizing the media schedule. The notion of an audience criterion needs to be mentioned here, though, for purposes of the current illustration.

7.3.2. IMPLEMENTING A REACH STRATEGY

As the reach rule states in Chapter 6, Section 6.3.1, a reach strategy should place just 1 or 2 insertions in each of many different vehicles that do not overlap much. Three of the vehicles in Table 7.1 are *FRIENDS*, *Seinfeld*, and *Frasier*, which are comedies and would be expected to have some overlap (this can be—and was—checked by examining the *between*-vehicle duplications). This suggests not using all three comedies in the final schedule. A reasonable starting point is to select only two of these three vehicles, namely the two with highest FIR, which are *FRIENDS* and *Seinfeld*.

Another two *apparently* similar programs are *60 Minutes* and *20/20*; although they are not usually scheduled at the same time, they often have similar content. However, their *actual* between-vehicle duplication is quite low—people tend to view one or the other (if at all), giving these two shows low overlap. Both are therefore included.

There are three evening news shows in the table, all of which must have low overlap because they are scheduled at the same time. The network news shows are therefore ideal for gaining high reach.

Media Mania (the Canonical Model) was then employed, using the reach rule, to estimate the reach for various combinations of the selected programs. Working within the budget, it was found that 1 insertion could be placed in 11 different programs of the original 13, only omitting *Frasier* (omitted earlier) and *David Letterman*. The resulting media schedule, given in Table 7.2 (first column), produces a respectable target group R1+/4 weeks of 75.5 percent. An option within Media Mania is to automatically find the media plan with the highest 1+ reach (see Section 7.4 and the Appendix, Section 2.5). Using this feature, it was found that the maximum possible R1+/4 weeks obtainable, keeping within the budget, is 75.7 percent, only fractionally higher than that achieved by using the reach rule. The optimal schedule (not shown) is very similar to the one selected strategically and uses 10 vehicles, omitting *Frasier* and *David Letterman*, along with *NYPD Blue*.

TABLE 7.2. Media plans using, respectively, the reach rule and the frequency rule

Program	Reach-strategy insertions	Frequency-strategy insertions
FRIENDS	1	0
Monday Night Football	1	6
Seinfeld	1	0
60 Minutes	1	0
ABC News	1	0
NBC Nightly News	1	0
20/20	1	6
CBS Evening News	1	0
Frasier	0	0
NYPD Blue	1	0
Financial Matters	1	0
David Letterman	0	0
Larry King	1	0
R1+/4 wks	75.5%	52.3%
R3+/4 wks	12.4%	27.6%
Total Cost	$399,500	$399,000
GRPs	129	168

7.3.3. IMPLEMENTING A FREQUENCY STRATEGY

Suppose that the media strategy for BMW calls for an MEF/c of 3 exposures, per 4 weeks (the MEF value of 3 was chosen because Media Mania automatically calculates an R3+ percentage; it could be any other value). The strategic rule's recommendations for gaining high frequency are almost the opposite of those for getting high reach. As the frequency rule states in Chapter 6, Section 6.3.2, it is desirable to have vehicles with high between-vehicle duplication, but especially those with high *within*-vehicle duplication. It is almost always the case that within-vehicle duplication for a particular vehicle will exceed the between-vehicle duplication of that vehicle with any other vehicle. Hence, the frequency strategy will tend to concentrate the insertions in just a few vehicles, but place many insertions in those vehicles.

The earlier table, Table 7.1, indicates which vehicles these should be. As can be seen from column 4 of that table, *Monday Night Football* has the highest within-vehicle duplication, or repeat-viewing loyalty. It also has a high FIR (and a relatively low CPMT for that matter), making it extremely attractive. Indeed, it might seem reasonable to place as many insertions as possible in *Monday Night Football* and have no other vehicles in the media plan. Media Mania shows that such a strategy would result in 9 insertions in *Monday Night Football*, giving an R3+ for the 4-week period of 20.6 percent. However, selecting a single vehicle ignores the potential benefits of between-vehicle duplication, so a second vehicle was selected to examine whether the 3+ reach of 20.6 percent could be improved. (Practically, too, there may be a limit of 2 insertions per week in Monday Night Football, which would force the addition of another program.)

Choosing the next vehicle is not as straightforward as the choice of *Monday Night Football*, because there are several other programs which have relatively high within-vehicle duplications. *FRIENDS* seems like a good candidate except that it does not have a very high duplication with *Monday Night Football*, probably because *FRIENDS* appeals slightly more to women than men (determined from program ratings by demographic groups). All of the network news shows have high within-vehicle duplications and high ratings, but they also have high cost, meaning that it may be too expensive to place many insertions in these programs (again, however, more correctly, profit should be the main consideration here). The same can be said of *Seinfeld, Frasier* and *NYPD Blue*. This leaves *60 Minutes* and *20/20*. Using Media Mania, insertions were juggled between *Monday Night Football* and either *60 Minutes* or *20/20*. The highest R3+/4 weeks was obtained with 6 insertions in each of *Monday Night Football* and *20/20*. The Media Mania results for this plan are given in Table 7.2 (second column). The R3+/4 weeks is 27.6 percent, being much higher than (relatively, a 34 percent improvement upon) the earlier value of 20.6 percent for the campaign having all its insertions in *Monday Night Football*. Also note that the reach (R1+) of the frequency strategy is only 52.3 percent, considerably below that obtained for the reach strategy, as expected.

Although CPMT was dismissed as the initial focus when selecting vehicles in Section 7.3.1 earlier, it turns out that CPMTs are useful when trying to achieve a frequency strategy (but not so much for a reach strategy). This is because the crux of a good frequency strategy is multiple insertions. The 12 insertions cost $399,000 in the above schedule, whereas they would have cost over $500,000 in *Seinfeld* or *Letterman*, well beyond the monthly budget of $400,000, and with lower effective (R3+) reach. Certainly you can have more insertions in a lower-cost vehicle, but this must be traded off against audience size, hence the value of CPMTs. This is evidenced from Table 7.1, where it can be seen that the lowest CPMTs occur for *20/20*, *60 Minutes*, and *Monday Night Football*, in that order. It transpired that these three vehicles were the key ones for developing the frequency strategy in this application.

7.3.4. COMPARING THE TWO STRATEGIES

Table 7.2 showed the best media plans for the respective reach and frequency strategies. Both campaigns have about the same number of insertions (11 and 12, respectively) and both spend very close to the budgeted amount of $400,000 for the 4-week advertising cycle. However, as might be expected, the high-reach strategy has the higher 1+ reach (75.5 percent compared with 52.3 percent), while the high-frequency strategy has the higher 3+ reach (27.6 percent compared with 12.4 percent). Not surprisingly, the costs per effective reach point (CPERPs) are vastly different. For the reach strategy, effective reach is R1+/4 weeks, and CPERP is $5291 for the high-reach plan but $7629 for the high-frequency plan. For the high-frequency strategy, effective reach is R3+/4 weeks, and CPERP is more than halved for the high-frequency plan, at $14,456, versus $32,217 for the high-reach plan (CPERP is, of course, much higher when more exposures are required to make the reach effective). By translating 1 percent of the target group into numbers and dividing CPERP by that number, the monthly cost of effectively reaching each target-group individual can be obtained.

A clear illustration of the overall difference between the two strategies (the two schedules) is exhibited in Figure 7.1. This graph compares the full frequency distribution for each strategy's schedule, giving the percentage of the target group exposed at each frequency level. The reach strategy starts off higher than the frequency strategy at the 1+ level, and the 2+ frequency levels are nearly the same. However, from the 3+ level onwards, the frequency strategy has substantially higher exposure levels. Indeed, the reach strategy has less than 0.5 percent of the target group exposed beyond the 5+ level, whereas the frequency strategy has nearly 30 percent. (A new model launch in the very competitive automobile market might well begin with an MEF/4-weekly of 10+. If so, it is evident that a *much bigger budget* than $400,000 per month would be required—to pay for many more insertions. The frequency rule would still be applied to best schedule these insertions to maximize R10+/4-weekly, just as it was applied in the R3+ case.)

As expected, the mix of insertions and number of vehicles selected for the two strategies are very different. The reach strategy has at most 1 insertion in 11 different vehicles whereas the frequency strategy uses only two vehicles, each having multiple insertions. These are precisely the types of insertion patterns that the strategic rules of Chapter 6 would predict for the reach and frequency strategies, respectively, which supports the validity of these qualitative guidelines for media scheduling. Also notice that the frequency strategy has higher GRPs, 168 compared with 129. This demonstrates yet again that GRPs are too blunt to form the basis of advanced media planning.

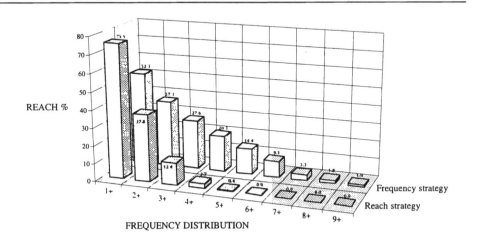

Figure 7.1. Frequency distributions (exposure distributions) for the high-reach strategy and the high-frequency strategy.

A reach-plus-frequency strategy (reach and frequency rule) could easily be implemented with Media Mania. For BMW, for instance, the objective of such a media plan might be to maximize monthly R2+ (reach at a frequency level of 2 or more per 4-week cycle) or more precisely R2-3 per month (those reached 2 to 3 times exactly). Although not shown here, the best schedule employs, as expected, somewhat more vehicles than the frequency plan but with more insertions in each than the single insertions in the reach plan.

This section has illustrated some of the capabilities of Media Mania. To experience the full range of capabilities, the reader should examine the other three examples given in Section 2.8 of the Appendix. These include a cross-media implementation.

7.4. Optimizing Schedules

As mentioned at the beginning of this chapter, there are many thousands and possibly millions of media schedules that a planner could develop. This number gets larger multiplicatively as the budget grows or as the number of available media vehicles increases. Obviously it is impossible for a media planner to try out all these possible schedules, so mathematical optimization is necessary. In this context, the planner must maximize one or more of the media plan's parameters (such as reach) subject to a budget constraint. Early work in this field was done by Little and Lodish (1966, 1969) and Aaker (1975). Rust (1986, chapter 5) gives a full review. Some recently developed commercial optimizers for television schedules include two British-developed packages named SuperMidas and X*Pert (these are direct matching methods which don't use a model). In addition, many ad agencies have their own in-house optimizers.

Media Mania incorporates an optimization algorithm, the technical details of which are reported in Danaher (1991b). The algorithm falls into the category known as "greedy heuristics," whereby each vehicle is selected in turn, an insertion is tentatively placed in it, and the vehicle which gives the greatest gain in audience criterion (effective reach per cycle) per unit cost has an *actual* insertion placed in it. This process is repeated until the entire budget has been spent. Danaher (1991b) shows that this method works very well in practice. While the heuristic algorithm employed by Media Mania is very fast, it can still take a long time if the budget is very large and many vehicles (20 or more) are available. An alternative in such situations is Rust's (1985) VIDEAC method, which takes about 15 minutes on a PC and has the additional advantage of requiring only vehicle ratings (or target group) FIRs as inputs (it calculates duplications via regression). Another good optimizer for very large schedules, which does not use a model, is Craig and Ghosh's (1985, 1993) exact direct matching method. Unfortunately, details of this method have not been made publicly available.

To implement schedule optimization, costs per insertion are required. Approximate costs can be obtained from ADWEEK's *Marketer's Guide to Media* (published twice a year) as a starting point. The actual cost paid is usually a negotiated price and depends on the volume of advertising involved and the competitive demand for the advertising time or space. To accommodate the actual cost, typical expected discounts can be factored into Media Mania (and other programs) quite easily by allowing the input cost per insertion to be reduced as more insertions are made in the vehicle.

Media Mania, as currently formulated, offers optimization of 1+ reach or 3+ reach per time period (R1+/c or R3+/c); see Appendix, Section 2.5. The selection of 1+ reach is perhaps obvious because the media planner usually wants to know what the "maximum reach" would be with a set of vehicles and insertions even if this is not the criterion for a particular plan. The selection of 3+ reach as the other optimization criterion is more arbitrary. It would be very time-consuming to run the program if Media Mania were programmed to optimize at many different effective reach levels, so the popular level of 3+ was chosen (this is not in any way to endorse it as an "effective" level in all circumstances, as Chapter 3's explanation of MEF/c should make clear). Moreover, note that the "c," the advertising cycle duration, can *vary* (a factor that is usually not specified in popular applications of "3+"). This realization gives the media planner considerable flexibility in maximizing effective reach, because effective reach, like MEF, is essentially a *rate* of exposures or OTSs.

By careful consideration of the timing of the vehicles that are candidates for the schedule, and the allowable number of insertions per time period (such as per program for a TV show or per issue for a monthly magazine), it is possible to optimize on 1+ reach or 3+ reach for a chosen duration of c: per *day*, per *week*, per *2 weeks*, *3 weeks*, or *4 weeks*, and so forth, as desired. For example, suppose that MEF/c was estimated to be 4+/4-weekly cycle. The media planner could achieve this *rate* by optimizing 3+ reach/ *3-weekly* and then, using the same vehicles selected by that optimization and following the same pattern of insertions, adding insertions for a further week until the 4-week budget amount is spent. Because this "variation of c" method is approximate rather than exact, it is very important to adhere to the relevant *strategic rule* when making this type of projection. The resulting 4+/4-week effective reach can then be calculated without optimization, with the expectation that it is quite close to optimal.

In summary, Media Mania allows sufficient optimization flexibility for most media planning applications. It is also easy to use (see Appendix) and accurate, with its Canonical Expansion and Approximate Log-linear model options.

7.5. Media Budget Setting

The media budget is usually set beforehand for the overall campaign. For instance, some overall method must have been used to produce the budget of $400,000 per 4 weeks for the BMW example, although no further details are given, such as whether this is a constant monthly budget for the year. A surprisingly large number of advertisers employ simplistic advertising-to-sales (A/S) ratio methods to set the overall budget, such as a fixed percent of last year's sales, or a fixed percent of this year's expected sales, or, in a slightly more complex variation of the A/S ratio method, setting expected "share of voice" (share of total category advertising expenditure) equal to expected share of market (market share). Several methods with a much better rationale, for new products and established products, are reviewed in Rossiter and Percy (1997, chapter 2).

Among the methods always recommended is the *task method*. Leading advertisers in both industrial and consumer categories report using this method (although its implementation probably varies in quality) as it is the most logical and defensible budget-setting method.

The procedures that have been advocated throughout this book can be used to provide a task-method check "in reverse"—that is, to see whether the spending rate is adequate to meet the pre-set sales goal for the brand. An example will show how this works, using the high-frequency plan for BMW from Table 7.2 earlier.

Recall that effective reach is based on maximizing the prospective customer's "disposition," or probability of purchase of the brand (Chapter 3). The figures showed that a 4-week spend of $400,000 (actually $399,000) would generate an effective reach for that month of 27.6 percent of the target group. This means 27.6 percent of the target group number should be "ready to buy" a BMW—assuming that the advertising "creative" has been persuasive. Of course, this doesn't mean that 27.6 percent of them *will* buy. Their favorable disposition has to carry forward into a showroom visit and a successful offer from the BMW salesperson. This is where the task method comes in. The task method (for this particular type of product) requires an estimate of two further probabilities: the probability that an effectively-reached prospect will visit the showroom, and the probability that the average BMW salesperson will convert the visit to a sale. Thus, the whole equation is: number in target group × effective reach proportion × p visit × p conversion = sales that month. (For simplification, this assumes that people outside the target group are not influenced by the advertising, and that the advertising is the only source of visitors, but these other factors can, if necessary, also be estimated by the task method.) Suppose, for illustration purposes, that BMW's market-survey tracking data indicate that 1 in 20 of those "aware" of the BMW automobile from the advertising (effectively reached) will actually make a visit, thus p visit = .05. Further, suppose that BMW's retail data show a conversion rate of 1 in 3 visitors, thus p conversion = .33. The equation now becomes: number in target group × .276 × .05 × .33 = number in target group × .0045; in other words, between 4 and 5 individuals per thousand of the target group could be expected to buy. Whether this is enough to meet BMW's targeted sales level (for the month or, projected, for the year) can then be assessed. Perhaps BMW wanted double that rate of purchase. Other things staying constant, the monthly effective reach would also have to be doubled, to 55.2 percent. This may not require exactly twice the monthly spend, however, and Media Mania could be used to find out what the most efficiently-attained R3+/4-weekly of 55.2 percent would cost.

Unfortunately, as currently formulated, Media Mania cannot go from a reach or effective reach target percentage "back" to the lowest-cost schedule of insertions. Accordingly, you have to use trial and error and try increasing the insertions by, say, 50 percent, 60 percent and so forth, according to the same *strategic rule*, and being careful to watch for insertion limits in vehicles per time period. In practice, this method is not too difficult unless the schedule of vehicles and insertions is unusually large to begin with. With the BMW schedule, for instance, it would be possible to use this method.

A final refinement is to estimate the *profitability* of the media plan. For this, it is necessary to plan in terms of numbers rather than percentages. Suppose that the gross profit per BMW sale is $5000. The profit from the media plan depends on the number of people in the target group. It was estimated earlier that the 27.6 percent effective reach of the 4-week plan would produce 4.5 sales per thousand people in the target group. Therefore: profit = number in target group × .0045 × $5000 – $399,000. The required size of the target group if the media plan is to break even is therefore $399,000 / $22.50 = 17,733 individuals. Verifying, these 17,733 individuals would be expected to result in 17,733 × .0045 = 79.8 cars being sold, which at $5000 profit per car is $399,000 in revenue, equal to the cost of the media plan. Thus, for a target group number above about 18,000 individuals, about 80 or more cars would be sold and this particular media plan for BMW would represent profitable advertising.

In many cases, it should be noted, advertising is not profitable *alone*. However, advertising often plays a contributory role in the overall marketing communications mix comprising promotions, personal selling and publicity—as well as in maintaining price—and it may well be that the cost per sale *without* advertising is higher than when advertising is included. In this way it may be possible for advertising to be "necessary" even though it is not, in a direct or isolated sense, profitable. The contrast to this is direct-response (DR) advertising, which nearly always must pay for itself.

APPENDIX

MANUAL FOR MEDIA MANIA

Acknowledgement. This manual was written by Peter Danaher with the assistance of Michael Tantrum, who also wrote most of the computer code for the Media Mania software.

Note. Media Mania's software has been set up with British spelling and New Zealand media vehicles in the examples. However, it is usable in any country by substituting your own media vehicles and media data.

1. Introduction

Typefaces in This Manual and What They Mean
[ ]   Text enclosed in square brackets indicates a key to be pressed.
Bold   Text in bold face indicates an item to click on with the mouse.
italics   Text in italics indicates text to type from the keyboard.

1.1. INSTALLATION

Install Media Mania by following these steps (all users must do these):
   a. Get into DOS by double clicking the MS-DOS prompt (or go to the Start menu, select Programs then select the MS-DOS prompt).
   b. Change to the top level directory.
              Type   *cd * [Enter]
   c. Create a directory on your hard disk drive (usually C:) called medmania.
              Type   *md \medmania* [Enter]
   d. Copy all the files from the floppy disk into the directory you have created.
              Type   *copy a:*.* c:\medmania* [Enter]

Having completed steps a through d, the following steps are for *Windows 95* or *Windows 98* users.
   (i)   Open up **Windows Explorer** from the **Start** menu.
   (ii)   Select the Medmania directory.
   (iii) In the right-hand section of the Explorer box, you will see a file named **medmania.exe** (the executable file). The icon is colored red, green and blue. Notice that the file immediately below this one, called medmania.ico, has an identical icon. Do nothing with the medmania.ico file.
              Left click on the Medmania.exe file, then right click on the same file.
   (iv)   Go down the menu until you get to the **Create Shortcut** option.
              Left click on **Create Shortcut**
   (v)   A new icon called Shortcut to Medmania will appear at the bottom of the list of files.
              Drag the Medmania shortcut icon onto your desktop
   (vi)   If you want to put this shortcut into your Start menu, right click on **Start**, left click on **Open** and drag the Medmania shortcut into the folder called **Programs**.

Having completed steps a through d, the following steps are for *Windows 3.11* or earlier users.
   (i)   Start windows.
              Type   *win* [Enter]
   (ii)   Choose **New** from the File menu. (See your Windows manual if you are unsure how to do this.)
              Click on **Program Group**
              Click on **OK**
   (iii) In the Description line:
              Type   *Media Mania*

Click on **OK**
(iv) Choose **New** from the File menu again.
      Click on **Program Item**
      Click on **OK**
 (v) In the Description line:
      Type   *Media Mania*
(vi) In the Command line:
      Type   *C:\MEDMANIA\MEDMANIA.EXE*
      Click on **OK**

Installation is now complete.

1.2. GETTING STARTED

Probably you have had experience using Windows before using this software. If not, try one of the Microsoft tutorials.

Start Media Mania by either:

a. Double clicking the **Media Mania** icon on your desktop, or

b. Selecting the Media Mania shortcut from your Start menu

    You will be presented with a screen with the Media Mania logo in the background, and a box with instructions in it (see Figure 1). Click on the **OK** button when you have read the contents.

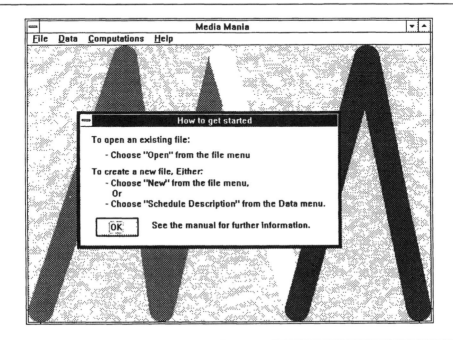

Figure 1. Getting started.

Now go to Section 2, Tutorial, to see how to use the Media Mania software.

2. Tutorial

Start the program up (if it isn't already running). See Section 1.2, Getting Started, if you are unsure how to do this.

This tutorial is divided into eight sections:

2.1. Creating datasets
2.2. Using existing datasets
2.3. Creating vehicle lists
2.4. Performing computations to construct schedules
2.5. Recalculating schedules and optimizing
2.6. Printing output
2.7. Ending Media Mania
2.8. Examples

2.1. CREATING DATASETS

In the context of this software, a dataset is a collection of vehicles (magazines, newspapers, television programs, etc.) containing information about readership/ viewership levels and advertising costs. Data for target groups are available from market research companies such as ACNielsen, Simmons and AGB.

There are two ways to create a dataset. Section 2.1.1 shows how to create a new dataset. Section 2.1.2 shows how to access data already stored in a file formatted as text (*.txt). Section 2.8 gives some examples of the use of these text files.

2.1.1. How to Create a New Dataset
   a. Firstly, click on **New** in the File menu (see Figure 2), then choose **Schedule Description** from the **Data** menu.
   b. Enter the information about the target audience and its size in the spaces provided, then click **OK**. Don't worry if you change your mind at a later stage, you can always come back and change the entries. (From now, you will be working with percentages of the target audience.)
   c. Now enter the information about the vehicles (see Figure 3). Pressing [Tab] takes you from one box to another, and [Shift][Tab] takes you back.
      "Name" is the name of the vehicle.
      "Code" is a unique three-letter code for the vehicle (used to save space when viewing the duplications).
      "F.I.R." is the first insertion reach (in percent form). For television programs this is the rating for each program, and for newspapers and magazines it is the single-issue readership.

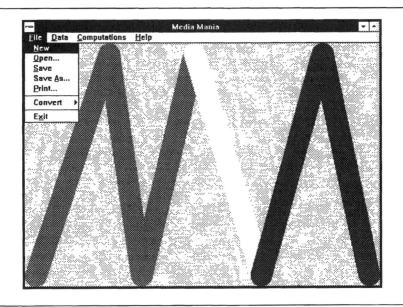

Figure 2. New file selection.

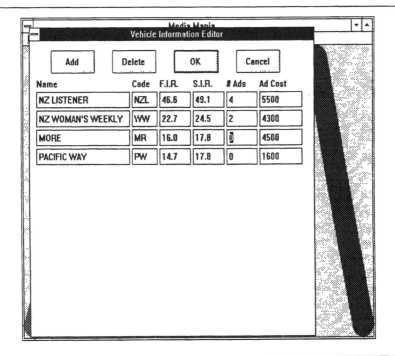

Figure 3. Vehicle information.

"S.I.R." is the second insertion reach (in percent form). This is the percentage of people in the target group reached when there are two insertions in successive episodes or issues of a vehicle. It is a function of within-vehicle duplication. Second insertion reach is always at least as big as the first insertion reach. S.I.R. is routinely reported in print surveys, but not often in TV surveys. If you do not know the within-vehicle duplication, you will need to approximate it by using the repeat-exposure figures reported in Chapter 6, Table 6.1. For example, if the TV program has an F.I.R. (rating) of 14 and it is an evening news program (which the table shows as having a day-to-day repeat-exposure proportion of 0.53), then the S.I.R. is $14 \times (2 - 0.53) = 20.6$. In general, S.I.R. = F.I.R. $\times$ (2 – repeat – exposure proportion).

"#Ads" is the number of insertions (advertisements) that you intend to place in the vehicle in total, that is, for the time period of this advertising cycle. Note that this is one insertion per episode or issue of the vehicle.

"Ad Cost" is the cost per insertion.

Click **Add** to add another vehicle, and click **Delete** to delete a vehicle

Click **OK** when you are finished

d. Now enter the Pairwise Duplication Values (in percent form). These are the between-vehicle duplications: the proportion of the target audience exposed to both of a pair of different vehicles. These figures are always reported in print surveys, but rarely in TV surveys or surveys with a mixture of media such as television and print. When working with TV or with a mixture of media, and duplications among vehicles are not known, an approximation can be obtained via the Duplication of Viewing Law. See Chapter 6, Sections 6.2.3 and 6.2.4.

e. Now you have finished entering data. This is a good time to save what you have done onto disk. To do this:

Choose **Save** from the File menu

2.1.2. *Selecting Vehicles from a Previously-created Dataset*

a. Choose **Vehicle Selection** from the Data menu.

b. Choose the file which contains the vehicles you want to include in your schedule (it will end in *.txt). Either double click on it, or click **OK**. A description of how to create these files is given in Section 2.3.

c. In the left-hand box you will see all the possible vehicles available from the file you chose (see Figure 4). The right-hand box is blank. Click on the vehicle(s) that you want in your schedule, then click on **Add**, one at a time.Or you can double click on the vehicle. The vehicle appears in the right-hand box.

d. If you decide that you don't want a vehicle after you have **Add**ed it, click on it (in the right-hand box), then click on **Delete**. Alternatively, you can double click on it (in the right-hand box). If you want to start over, click on **Clear**.

Click **OK** to finish

e. Now the program automatically takes you to step 2.1.1a (Schedule Description Editor), but you do not have to enter data as in steps b to d.

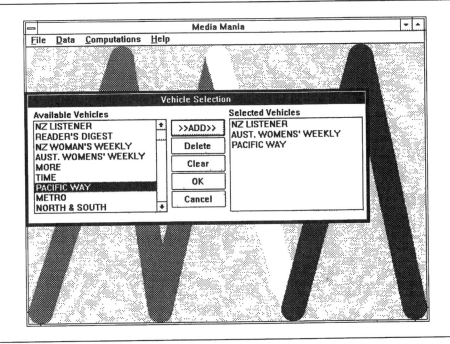

Figure 4. Vehicle selection from a previously-created dataset.

2.2. USING EXISTING DATASETS

Suppose that you have just started up Media Mania. You want to use a dataset that you created in a previous session, like the section above. The file is stored on disk, so all that is required is to open it. Choose **Open** from the File menu and choose the file you want (it will have a *.inf suffix).

2.3. CREATING VEHICLE LISTS

These lists are for use with the **Vehicle Selection** option in the Data menu, as explained above in Section 2.1.2. They are ASCII text files.

    a. Choose **Vehicle Name/Code Entry** from the Data menu.

    b. If you want to create a new file, click **Yes**, otherwise click **No**.

    c. If you clicked **No** above, you will be asked for the name of the file you want to modify.

    d. Enter data in the format shown, then either press [Enter], or click **Add**.

    e. Click **OK** when you have finished. You will be asked whether you want to save the changes.

2.4. PERFORMING COMPUTATIONS TO CONSTRUCT SCHEDULES

Now you are ready to construct media schedules from the dataset.

2.4.1. Choosing a Model

To perform the computations to construct a schedule, either choose **Canonical Model**, **Beta Binomial**, or **Approximate Log Linear** from the Computations menu. In order of accuracy the models are Approximate Log Linear, Canonical Model, and the Beta Binomial. In order of speed, they are the Beta Binomial, Canonical Model, and the Approximate Log Linear. These models were discussed in Chapter 7, Section 7.2.

One of the purposes of the Media Mania software is to allow you to compare alternative media exposure models. This can be achieved easily by selecting different models from the Computations menu. The **Approximate Log Linear** model is generally the most accurate of the three models and so should be treated as the benchmark model. However, this model becomes slow computationally when the number of vehicles exceeds six and there are 4 or more insertions in each vehicle. Therefore, it is not advisable to use the Approximate Log Linear model for large media schedules.

The **Beta Binomial** model is also very fast and the one most commonly used, but it suffers from overestimating reach, poorly approximating "lumpy" exposure distributions (especially for print campaigns), and the declining reach problem.

The default model is the **Canonical Model**, as it has both good speed and accuracy.

2.4.2. Results

Having selected the computation method (which will be the **Canonical Model** if you didn't make a choice), you should now be presented with a screen of Results. Figure 5 gives an example of the top half of the Results screen. The bottom half, which graphs the frequency distribution, is displayed by clicking on the right-hand sidebar.

The Results box has five buttons displayed across the top. The **Optimise** and **Recalc** buttons are explained in Section 2.5. The **Print** button will be explained in Section 2.6.

The **Raw Freq** button changes the exposure distribution output from a minimum-frequency distribution (1+, 2+, 3+, etc.) to a raw, exact-frequency distribution (exactly 1 exposure, exactly 2, etc.). For instance, instead of giving the percentage of people exposed 4 or more times in the schedule, it gives the percentage exposed exactly 4 times. This is instructive for seeing how lumpy the exposure distribution is, particularly for print campaigns, by using the Canonical Model or Approximate Log Linear. It may be remembered that Beta Binomial cannot handle lumpy distributions and always estimates them to be smooth.

2.5. RECALCULATING SCHEDULES AND OPTIMIZING

Now that you can see the Results for your initial media schedule, you will probably be asking questions such as: "What if I had placed more insertions in one vehicle, and fewer

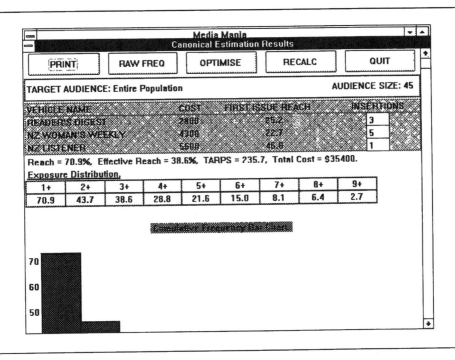

Figure 5. Results estimated by the Canonical Model.

in another? Would that have given me greater reach? What about the cost?" Insertion juggling allows you to ask these "What if?" questions. Here's how it's done.

a. Click in the box with the number of insertions you wish to change. Pressing [Tab] or [Shift][Tab] is another way of taking you from one box to another.
b. Enter the new number of insertions for the vehicle(s) you want to change.
c. Click on **Recalc**.
d. To see the theoretical optimum schedule of insertions given the budget, click on **Optimise** (this option is not available with the Approximate Log Linear Model). Figure 6 shows the screen available when this option is selected.
   You will be presented with a dialog box prompting you for various options.
e. Enter the budget.
f. Click on either **Reach** (R1+/c) or **Effective Reach** (R3+/c).
g. Click on either **Set to Zero** or **Manual Input** (to optimise Reach) or **Manual Input** (to optimise Effective Reach). If you clicked on Manual Input, then you will be presented with a screen with which to enter the minimum insertion levels. These are the levels which must be inserted for each vehicle. Don't start with all zeros when optimising Effective Reach. Also pay attention to quantity discounts. For example, if you require at least 3 insertions in *Reader's Digest* magazine to be eligible for a discount, then you would enter 3 in the box next to *Reader's Digest*.
h. Click **OK**.

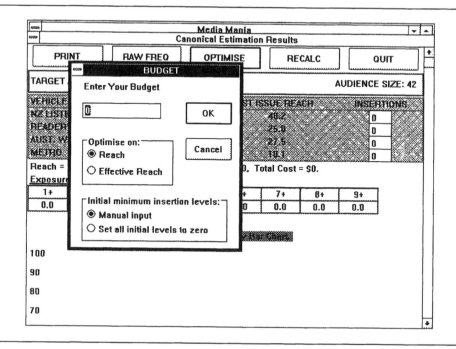

Figure 6. Optimizing the schedule of insertions in relation to budget.

i. Click in the box with the number of insertions you wish to change. Pressing [Tab] or [Shift][Tab] is another way of taking you from one box to another.
j. Enter the number of insertions that you want to change to.
k. Click on **OK**.

The Results from the Optimiser will be displayed. Click on **Raw Freq** to display the exact-frequency (k/c) exposure distribution, and click again to redisplay the minimum-frequency (k+/c) exposure distribution. Click on **Quit** to take you back to the menu.

2.6. PRINTING OUTPUT

Click on **Print** to print the Results to a system printer. You will see a dialog box appear, and various options are available to you. If you want to print to a file, click on **Print to file** in the bottom left-hand corner. If you want to print to a different printer than the current one, click on **Setup**. If you want to print the dataset, then go back to the menu, and choose **Print** from the File menu.

2.7. ENDING MEDIA MANIA

To quit from Media Mania:
    Choose **Exit** from the File menu.

2.8. EXAMPLES

There are three examples in this tutorial. The first is a TV campaign for BMW, the second is print campaign for Regaine, and the third is a combined TV and print campaign for AT&T. Each example uses realistic data, typically available from readership surveys and television people meter panels.

2.8.1. *BMW*

The target audience for this campaign is men aged 35+ years who live in urban areas and have high incomes. The media plan is solely television. The budget is $1,000,000, for each 4-week advertising cycle. Only one cycle's schedule is to be calculated. The objective is to maximise reach. This schedule could be repeated in spaced cycles in an awareness reach pattern.

- a. Choose **New** from the File menu.
- b. Choose **Vehicle Selection** from the Data menu.
- c. Double click on **bmw.txt** in the left-hand box.
- d. Choose **Frasier, NBC Nightly News, 60 Minutes, Financial Matters, Monday Night Football**, and **NYPD Blue**.
- e. Click **OK** when you have finished.
- f. Enter the target audience and size in the spaces provided. Click **OK**.
- g. Enter some insertion levels for the vehicles. Entered in this example are 8, 3, 1, 2, 4, 8 for *Frasier, NBC Nightly News, 60 Minutes, Financial Matters, Monday Night Football*, and *NYPD Blue*, respectively.
- h. Click **OK** when you have finished.
- i. Click **OK**.
- j. Choose **Canonical Model** from the Data menu.

The Results are given in Figure 7 and show that the reach (1+/4 weeks) is 71.9 percent and total cost is $999,000. The label TARPs refers to GRPs for the target audience. This is a good result, but can it be better? Experiment. See if you can get results higher than this.

- k. Now click on **Optimise**.
- l. Enter the budget of 1000000 (note: no commas).
- m. Click on **Reach**.
- n. Click on **Set all initial values to zero**.
- o. Click on **OK**.

The reach is now 73.0 percent, with a total cost of 998,000.

- p. Click on **Quit**.
- q. Select **Beta Binomial** from the Computations menu.
- r. Repeat all the above steps and compare the Results.
  Remember that you can get a printout of any of the Results.

2.8.2. *Regaine*

Regaine is a hair restorer. The target audience for this campaign is men aged between 25 and 49 years who are in the upper socio-economic bracket. The campaign is to be exclusively in print media. The budget for the campaign is set at $300,000, for a one-off advertising cycle lasting 3 months. The objective is to maximise effective reach.

a. Choose **New** from the File menu.

b. Choose **Vehicle Selection** from the Data menu.

c. Double click on **Regaine.txt** in the left-hand box.

d. Now pick some magazines that you think are likely to be good vehicles. In this example, the selections are **Reader's Digest**, **National Geographic**, **Time**, **Metro**, **Auto Age**, and **Sunday News**.

e. Click **OK** when you have finished.

f. Enter the target audience and size (in thousands) in the spaces provided.

g. Click **OK**.

h. Next, enter some insertion levels for the vehicles. Weigh up F.I.R. and S.I.R. against cost. Remember, the more magazines you have, the greater the reach; whereas the more insertions you have in fewer magazines, the greater the effective reach. Entered in this example are 3, 1, 3, 1, 2, 1 for *Reader's Digest*, *National Geographic*, *Time*, *Metro*, *Auto Age*, and *Sunday News*, respectively.

i. Click **OK** when you have finished.

j. Click **OK** for the Duplication Editor.

k. Choose **Canonical Model** from the Data menu.

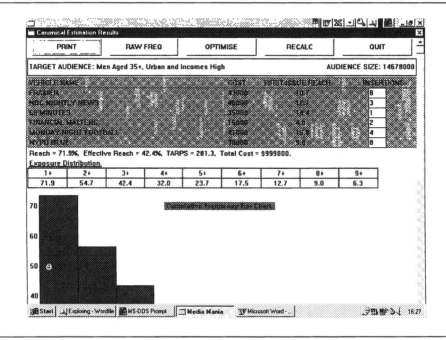

Figure 7. Results for the BMW campaign.

The Results show that the reach is 65.5 percent, the effective reach is 33.8 percent, and total cost is $272,500. There could be room for improvement for effective reach, and the budget hasn't been spent. Try changing vehicles, as follows.

l. **Add: Gentleman's Quarterly** and **TV Guide. Delete: National Geographic, Metro**, and **Auto Age**.

m. Enter as an alternative schedule 3, 1, 3, 1, 2 for *Gentleman's Quarterly, Reader's Digest, Time, TV Guide*, and *Sunday News*, respectively. Click on **Recalc**.

Reach has gone up to 79.9 percent but, more importantly, effective reach has gone up to 51.7 percent, and total cost is still below the budget of $300,000. Experiment. See if you can get effective (3+) reach higher than this. However, the example continues with these five vehicles.

n. Now click on **Optimise**.

o. Enter the budget of 300000 (note: no comma).

p. Click on **Reach**.

q. Click on **Set all initial values to zero**.

r. Click on **OK**.

Notice that the reach is now 80.9 percent but effective reach is down to 50.2 percent. Therefore, optimising on reach is not a good procedure. The total cost is $300,000.

s. Repeat the Optimise process for **Effective Reach**, and use the **Manual Input** (don't set all the initial insertion values to zero). Compare the Results.

t. Click on **Quit**.

u. Select **Beta Binomial** from the Computations menu.

v. Repeat all the above steps and compare the Results.

Remember that you can get a printout of any of the Results.

2.8.3. AT&T

Suppose that AT&T wants to advertise a new call-waiting service. The target audience for this campaign is women aged between 18 and 39 who live in urban areas and have medium to high household incomes. Two media types that have good reach for this female target audience are TV and women's magazines, and AT&T has decided to use both. The total budget for the campaign is $1,000,000, to be spent in a single 2-week blitz. The ads are direct-response ads and you want to maximise reach.

a. Choose **New** from the File menu.

b. Choose **Vehicle Selection** from the Data menu.

c. Double click on **att.txt** in the left-hand box.

d. Choose **Friends, Seinfeld, NBC Nightly News, XFiles, NYPD Blue, Cosmopolitan, Family Circle**, and **Woman's Day**.

e. Click **OK** when you have finished.

f. Enter the target audience and size in the spaces provided. Click **OK**.

g. Enter insertion levels of 2, 2, 2, 2, 2, 2, 2, 2 for *Friends, Seinfeld, NBC Nightly News, XFiles, NYPD Blue, Cosmopolitan, Family Circle*, and *Woman's Day*, respectively.

h. Click **OK** when you have finished.

i. Click **OK**.

j. Choose **Canonical Model** from the Data menu.

The Results show that the reach is 66.9 percent, and total cost is $981,000.

k. **Optimise** on **Reach**.

The reach is now 68.8 percent, with a cost of $985,000.

Now, suppose that the network showing *Friends* offers a discount for 4 or more insertions, bringing the price per insertion down to $75,000. This would only be worth taking advantage of if it gives better Results than with fewer than 4 insertions in the *Friends*. To try this:

l. Click on **Quit**.

m. Choose **Vehicle Information** from the Data menu.

n. Change the ad cost for *Friends* to 75000, and the insertion level to 4.

o. Click **OK**.

p. Click **OK**.

q. Choose **Canonical Model** from the Data menu.

r. Click **Optimise**.

s. Enter the budget, and set the reach and manual input buttons. Click **OK**.

t. Enter 4, 0, 0, 0, 0, 0, 0, 0 as the minimum levels, and click **OK**.

The Results show that reach is now 69.0 percent and the total cost is now $979,000. While the reach has not increased much, you have lowered the cost by $6000. Therefore, there is some benefit in taking advantage of the discount.

REFERENCES

Aaker D.A. (1975) ADMOD: An advertising decision model. *Journal of Marketing Research*, 12(1), 37-55.

Aaker D.A. and Carman J.C. (1982) Are you overadvertising? *Journal of Advertising Research*, 22(4), 57-70.

Achenbaum, A.A. (1977) Effective exposure, a new way of evaluating media. Paper presented at the Association of National Advertisers' Media Workshop, Association of National Advertisers, Inc., New York.

Adams, A.J. and Blair, M.H. (1992) Persuasive advertising and sales accountability: past experience and forward validation. *Journal of Advertising Research*, 32(2), 20-25.

ADWEEK (1994) *Marketer's Guide to Media*. ADWEEK, L.P., New York, 17(1), whole issue.

Artz, E.L. (1991) The lifeblood of brands. *Advertising Age*, November 4, p. 32.

Assael, H. and Poltrack, D.F. (1991) Using single-source data to select TV programs based on purchasing behavior. *Journal of Advertising Research*, 31(4), 9-17.

Assael, H. and Poltrack, D.F. (1993) Using single-source data to select TV programs based on purchasing behavior: Part II. *Journal of Advertising Research*, 33(1), 58-56.

Assael, H. and Poltrack, D.F. (1994) Can demographic profiles of heavy users serve as a surrogate for purchase behavior in selecting TV programs? *Journal of Advertising Research*, 34(1), 11-17.

Baker K., Harris, P., and O'Brien, J. (1989) Data fusion: an appraisal and experimental evaluation. *Journal of the Market Research Society*, 31(2), 153-212.

Barwise, T.P. (1986) Repeat-viewing of prime-time TV series. *Journal of Advertising Research*, 26(4), 9-14.

Beed, T.W. (1992) An overview of the transition from diary-based television audience measurement to people meters in Australia and New Zealand. In *Proceedings of the ESOMAR/ARF Worldwide Electronic and Broadcast Audience Research Symposium*, Toronto, ESOMAR, Amsterdam, pp. 139-162.

Blattberg, R.C. and Jeuland, A.P. (1980) Micromodelling of the advertising-sales relationship. In R.P. Bagozzi, K.L. Bernhardt, P.S. Busch, D.W. Cravens, J.F. Hair, Jr., and C.A. Scott (Eds), *AMA Educator's Proceedings*, American Marketing Association, Chicago, pp. 302-306.

Broadbent, S. (1979) *Spending Advertising Money* (3rd edn). Business Books Ltd, London.

Broadbent, S. (1984) Modelling with adstock. *Journal of the Market Research Society*, 26(4), 295-312.

Broadbent, S. (1996) The gatekeeper takes the lie-detector test. *Admap*, December, 34-39.

Broadbent, S. and Fry, T. (1995) Adstock modelling for the long term. *Journal of the Market Research Society*, 37(4), 385-403.

Brown, G. (1992) Diary measurement of radio listening. *Journal of the Market Research Society*, 35(3), 201-215.

Brown, G. (1994) The awareness problem: attention and memory effects from TV and magazine advertising. *Admap*, January, 15-20.

Cannon, H.M. and Seamons, B.L. (1995) Simulating single-source data: how it fails us just when we need it most. *Journal of Advertising Research*, 35(6), 53-62.

Carpenter, G.S. and Nakamoto, K. (1989) Consumer preference formation and pioneering advantage. *Journal of Marketing Research*, 26(3), 285-298.

Chandon, J-L.J. (1976) A comparative study of media exposure models. Ph.D. *dissertation*, Northwestern University, Evanston, Illinois.

Colman, S. and Brown G. (1983) Advertising tracking studies and sales effects. *Journal of the Market Research Society*, 25(2), 165-183.

Cowling, T. (1997) New data links for better targeting and planning. *Admap*, February, 28-31.

Craig, C.S. and Ghosh, A. (1985) Maximizing effective reach in media planning. In R.F. Lusch, G.T. Ford, G.L. Frazier, R.D. Howell, C.A. Ingene, M. Reilly, and R.W. Stampfl (Eds), *AMA Educator's Proceedings*, American Marketing Association, Chicago, pp. 78-182.

Craig, C.S. and Ghosh, A. (1993) Using household-level viewing data to maximize effective reach. *Journal of Advertising Research*, 33(1), 38-47.

Danaher, P.J. (1988) A log-linear model for predicting magazine audiences. *Journal of Marketing Research*, 25(5), 356-362.

Danaher, P.J. (1989) An approximate log-linear model for predicting magazine audiences. *Journal of Marketing Research*, 26(5), 573-579.

Danaher, P.J. (1991a) A canonical expansion model for multivariate media exposure distributions: a generalization of the "duplication of viewing law." *Journal of Marketing Research*, 28(3), 361-367.

Danaher, P.J. (1991b) Optimizing response functions of media exposure distributions. *Journal of the Operational Research Society*, 52(7), 537-552.

Danaher, P.J. (1992) Some statistical modelling problems in the advertising industry. *The American Statistician*, 56(5), 255-260.

Danaher, P.J. and Beed, T.W. (1993) A coincidental survey of peoplemeter panelists: comparing what people say with what they do. *Journal of Advertising Research*, 33(1), 86-92.

Danaher, P.J. and Green, B.J. (1997) A comparison of media factors that influence the effectiveness of direct response television advertising. *Journal of Direct Marketing*, 11(2), 46-58.

Danaher, P.J. and Rust, R.T. (1992) Linking segmentation studies. *Journal of Advertising Research*, 32(3), 18-23.

Day, G.S. (1971) Attitude change, media and word-of-mouth. *Journal of Advertising Research*, 11(6), 31-40.

Donthu, N. (1994) Double jeopardy in program choice. *Journal of the Academy of Marketing Science*, 22(2), 180-185.

Ebbinghaus, H. (1885) *Memory*. Duncker, Leipzig.

Ehrenberg, A.S.C. and Wakshlag, J. (1987) Repeat-viewing with people meters. *Journal of Advertising Research*, 27(1), 9-13.

Ephron, E. (1995) More weeks, less weight: the shelf-space model of advertising. *Journal of Advertising Research*, 35(3), 18-23.

Eskin, G.J. (1985) Tracking advertising and promotion performance with single-source data. *Journal of Advertising Research*, 25(1), 31, 33-39.

Eskin, G.J. and Baron, P.H. (1977) Effects on price and advertising in test market experiments. *Journal of Marketing Research*, 14(4), 499-508.

Fox, R.J., Reddy, S.K., and Rao, B. (1997) Modeling response to repetitive promotional stimuli. *Journal of the Academy of Marketing Science*, 25(3), 242-255.

Garfinkle, N. (1963) A marketing approach to media selection. *Journal of Advertising Research*, 3(4), 7-15.

Givon, M. and Horsky, D. (1990) Untangling the effects of purchase reinforcement and advertising carryover. *Marketing Science*, 9(2), 171-187.

Goodhardt, G.J. and Ehrenberg, A.S.C. (1969) Duplication of television viewing between and within channels. *Journal of Marketing Research*, 6(2), 169-178.

Goodhardt, G.J., Ehrenberg, A.S.C., and Collins, M.A. (1987) *The Television Audience: Patterns of Viewing* (2nd edn). Gower, London.

Green, A. (1997) Media research in the Asia-Pacific region. *Admap*, February, 46-49.

Gullen, P. and Johnson, H. (1986) Product purchasing and TV viewing: measuring and relating the two. In New Developments in Media Research, ESOMAR, Amsterdam, pp. 345-363.

Haley, R.I. (1978) Sales effects of media weight. *Journal of Advertising Research*, 18(3), 9-18.

Headen, R.S., Klompmaker, J.E., and Rust, R.T. (1979) The duplication of viewing law and television media schedule evaluation. *Journal of Marketing Research*, 16(4), 333-340.

Helsen, K. and Schmittlein, D.C. (1992) How does a product market's typical price promotion pattern affect timing of household's purchases? An empirical study using UPC scanner data. Journal of Retailing, 68(3), 316-338.

Herr, P.M., Kardes, F.R., and Kim, J. (1991) Effects of word-of-mouth and product-attribute information on persuasion: an accessibility-diagnosticity perspective. *Journal of Consumer Research*, 17(4), 454-462.

Holmes, J.H. and Lett, J.D. (1977) Product sampling and word-of-mouth. *Journal of Advertising Research*, 17(5), 35-40.

Howard, J.A. (1977) *Consumer Behavior: Application of Theory*. McGraw-Hill, New York.

Jones, J.P. (1995) Single-source research begins to fulfill its promise. *Journal of Advertising Research*, 35(3), 9-16.

Jones, J.P. (1997) What does effective frequency mean in 1997? *Journal of Advertising Research*, 37(4), 14-20.

Kent, R.A. (1995) *Measuring Media Audiences*. London, Routledge.

Leckenby, J.D. and Rice, M.D. (1985) A beta binomial network TV exposure model using limited data. *Journal of Advertising*, 14(3), 25-31.

Leckenby, J.D. and Rice, M.D. (1986) The declining reach phenomenon in exposure distribution models. *Journal of Advertising*, 15(3), 13-20.

Leone, R.P. (1995) Generalizing what is known about temporal aggregation and advertising carryover. *Marketing Science*, 14(3, Part 2), G141-G150.

Little, J.D.C. (1979) Aggregate advertising models: the state of the art. *Operations Research*, 27(4), 630-667.

Little, J.D.C. and Lodish, L.M. (1966) A media selection model and its optimization by dynamic programming. *Industrial Management Review*, 8(1), 15-23.

Little, J.D.C. and Lodish, L.M. (1969) A media planning calculus. *Operations Research*, 17(1), 1-35.

Lodish L.M. and Lubetkin, B. (1992) General truths? Nine key findings from IRI test data. *Admap*, February, 9-15.

Longman, K.A. (1971) *Advertising*. New York: Harcourt Brace Jovanovich.

Mahajan, V. and Muller, E. (1986) Advertising pulsing policies for generating awareness of new products. *Marketing Science*, 5(2), 89-111.

Mazur, J.E. (1994) *Learning and Behavior* (3rd edn). Prentice-Hall, Englewood Cliffs, New Jersey.

McDonald, C. (1971) What is the short-term effect of advertising? *Special Report No. 71-142*, Marketing Science Institute, Cambridge, Massachusetts.

McDonald, C. (1996a) *Advertising Reach and Frequency* (2nd edn). NTC Business Books, Lincolnwood, Illinois.

McDonald, C. (1996b) Advertising sales effects. *Admap*, April, 39-43.

McDonald, C. (1996c) How frequently should you advertise? *Admap*, July-August, 22-25.

Mesak, H.I. (1992) An aggregate advertising pulsing model with wearout effects. *Marketing Science*, 11(3), 310-325.

Metheringham, R.A. (1964) Measuring the net cumulative coverage of a print campaign. *Journal of Advertising Research*, 4(4), 23-28.

Midgley, D.F. and Dowling, G.R. (1978) Innovativeness: the concept and its measurement. *Journal of Consumer Research*, 4(4), 229-242.

Midgley, D.F. and Dowling, G.R. (1993) A longitudinal study of product form innovation: the interaction between predispositions and social messages. *Journal of Consumer Research*, 19(4), 611-625.

Midgley, D.F., Morrison, P.D., and Roberts, J.H. (1992) The effect of network structure in industrial diffusion processes. Research Policy, 21(6), 533-552.

Millward Brown (1992) *People, Brands & Advertising*. Millward Brown International Plc., Leamington Spa, England.

Moran, W.T. (1976) Insights from pricing research. Paper presented at the Marketing Conference of The Conference Board, New York.

Moran, W.T. (1978) The advertising-promotion balance. Paper presented at the Association of National Advertisers' Advertising Research Workshop, New York.

Naples, M.J. (1979) *Effective Frequency: The Relationship Between Frequency and Advertising Effectiveness*. Association of National Advertisers, Inc., New York.

National Infomercial Marketing Association (1994) Study reported in USA Today, October 21-23, p. 1A.

Ozga, S.A. (1960) Imperfect markets through lack of knowledge. *Quarterly Journal of Economics*, 74(1), 29-52.

Peckham, J.O. (1981) *The Wheel of Marketing*. Self-published, Scarsdale, New York.

Pincott, G. (1990) Investigating readership lag. Proprietary report, Millward Brown Plc., Leamington Spa, England.

Priemer, A.B. (1986) New alternatives to effective frequency and media planning. *Journal of Media Planning*, 1(1), 25-28.

Priemer, A.B. (1987) Overcoming obstacles to professionalism in media planning. *Journal of Media Planning*, 2(2), 5-11.

Priemer, A.B. (1989) *Effective Media Planning*. Lexington Books, Lexington, Massachusetts.

Priemer, A.B. (1990) Finding the forest in media planning. *Journal of Media Planning*, 5(2), 7-12.

Reichel, W. and Wood, L. (1997) Recency in media planning—re-defined. *Journal of Advertising Research*, 37(4), 66-74.

Rice, M.D. and Leckenby, J.D. (1986) An empirical test of a proprietary television media model. *Journal of Advertising Research*, 26(4), 17-21.

Roberts, A. (1994a) TV exposure, brand buying and ad effects. *Admap*, June, 31-37.

Roberts, A. (1994b) Media exposure and consumer purchasing: an improved data fusion technique. *Marketing and Research Today*, 22(3), 159-172.

Roberts, A. (1996) What do we know about advertising's short-term effects? *Admap*, February, 42-45.

Robertson, T.S. (1971) *Innovative Behavior and Communication*. Holt, Rinehart and Winston, New York.

Rossiter, J.R. and Percy, L. (1987) *Advertising & Promotion Management*. McGraw-Hill, New York.

Rossiter, J.R. and Percy, L. (1997) *Advertising Communications & Promotion Management* (2nd edn). The McGraw-Hill Companies, Inc., New York.

Rossiter, J.R., Percy, L,. and Donovan, R.J. (1991) A better advertising planning grid. *Journal of Advertising Research*, 31(5), 11-21.

Rust, R.T. (1985) Selecting network television advertising schedules. *Journal of Business Research*, 13(6), 483-494.

Rust, R.T. (1986) *Advertising Media Models: A Practical Guide*. Lexington Books, Lexington, Massachusetts..

Schroer, J.C. (1990) Ad spending: growing market share. *Harvard Business Review*, 68(1), 44-48.

Schultz, D.E. and Block, M.P. (1986) Empirical estimatation of advertising response functions. *Journal of Media Planning*, 1(1), 17-24.

Sheth, J.N. (1971) Word-of-mouth in low risk innovations. *Journal of Advertising Research*, 11(3), 15-18.

Simon, H. (1982) ADPULS: an advertising model with wearout and pulsation. *Journal of Marketing Research*, 19(3), 352-363.

Singh, S.N. and Rothschild, M.L. (1983) Recognition as a measure of learning from television commercials. *Journal of Marketing Research*, 20(3), 235-248.

Stankey, M.J. (1988) Using media more effectively. *Business*, April-June, 20-27.

Strong, E.C. (1977) The spacing and timing of advertising. *Journal of Advertising Research*, 17(6), 25-31.

Sutherland, M. (1993) *Advertising and the Mind of the Consumer*. Allen & Unwin, Sydney, Australia.

Urban, G., Carter, T., Gaskin, S.,and Mucha, Z. (1986) Market share rewards to pioneering brands. *Management Science*, 32(6), 645-659

Urban, G.L. and Hauser, J.R. (1993) *Design and Marketing of New Products* (2nd edn). Prentice Hall, Englewood Cliffs, New Jersey.

Urban, G.L. and von Hippel, E. (1988) Lead user analysis for the development of new industrial products. *Management Science*, 34(5), 569-582.

von Hippel, E. (1986) Lead users: a source of novel product concepts. *Management Science*, 32(7), 791-805.

Weinberg, C.B. (1994) Seminar presented at the Australian Graduate School of Management, Sydney, Australia.

Williamson, D.A. (1996) New ammo for click-rate debate. *Advertising Age*, August 19, p. 24.

Winter, F.W. (1980) Match target markets to media audiences. *Journal of Advertising Research*, 20(1), 61-66.

Woodside, A.G. (1994) Modeling linkage advertising: going beyond better media comparisons. *Journal of Advertising Research*, 34(4), 22-31.

Zielske, H. (1986) Using effective frequency in media planning. *Journal of Media Planning*, 1(1), 53-56.

INDEX

16.2